Hannah Brencher is one of the best, most poignant writers of our time, for our generation. In a world where we expect so much to happen so quickly, where we turn away from fear and from hard things, Hannah reminds us—in her beautiful, pointed, eloquent way—that the hard stuff is worth showing up for, worth fighting for, and worth working for. In reading her words, I was reminded how consistency and confidence are both learned and earned. And that the best things in life are often those we get a little bruised (and a little stronger) chasing after.

EMILY LEY, bestselling author of *Grace, Not Perfection* and *When Less Becomes More*

Here is the truth-telling, soul-strengthening rally cry for our generation. Through her refreshing vulnerability, empowering proclamations, and practical how-tos, Hannah Brencher gets real about fear and shame and exposes the truth of the victorious life available to us. You will finish this book with a newfound strength to keep showing up and a clarifying confidence in who you were created to be. Give this book to everyone you know who wants to fight for their fullest life and move forward in their purpose.

HOSANNA WONG, author, pastor, and spoken word artist

Hannah Brencher vividly walks us through our own lives as we press into the hard things. With grace and grit, she gives practical advice and tells moving stories that give you all you need in your toolbox to fix unhealthy patterns and continue to fight and show up in your life. This book is a message of ownership, encouragement, and challenge. I know you'll find yourself reading it several times. It's just *that* helpful!

CHELSEA CROCKETT HURST, author of *Above All Else* and *Your Own Beautiful*

Fighting Forward is the book we *all* needed—the book you'll want to read again and again. Get ready to be lifted up, set on a solid path, and cheered on with every turn of the page. Hannah Brencher has gifted us with an anthem for our weary souls that delivers vibrant hope, purpose, and needed truth!

LARA CASEY, author of *Cultivate* and *Make It Happen,* and CEO of Cultivate What Matters

Hannah Brencher has always had a way of writing the words I've needed in order to find my truth, identify my worthiness, and point me back to the person I'm meant to operate in this world as. As once a reader and distant fan and now a friend, I have been impacted by Hannah's ability to weave words around in an anthem song for everyone who reads it. You want *Fighting Forward* because everyone needs someone in their corner to remind them of all the reasons they can get back up—but it's also a read that feels like it's sitting in the mess with you. This book is not just a flashlight to get you out of the woods; it's also a mirror that holds the truths your soul needs to hear and the song that gets you up and teaches you to dance again.

ARIELLE ESTORIA, poet, author, speaker

Picture you, beaten up and feeling defeated, resting against the edge of the ring ready to quit. God enters, eager to fight for you, to help you see the strength he has given you. Because God is loving and kind, he pulls in his friend Hannah Brencher—the compassionate coach, guide, poet, and prophet—who is going to use his words to show you: you're already standing; God has already won; and the fighting is what we get to do. This book is for you.

JESS CONNOLLY, pastor, author of *You Are the Girl for the Job,* founder of Go + Tell Gals

Fighting Forward is brilliant—it's the book the world needs right now. Hannah Brencher is a compelling storyteller and an honest guide who will help you live a better story. She teaches us to fight fear and name the lies that hold us back. She helps us become a better version of ourselves, not because we need to for anyone else, but because we are worth it. She will help you get unstuck and fight for the life you're meant to live.

ALLI WORTHINGTON, author of *Standing Strong,* business coach, cofounder of Called Creatives

I love how Hannah Brencher crafted this book. Not only will you feel motivated as you read, but the vivid storytelling and imagery mean that one day when you find yourself far away from your copy and in need of a pep talk from your friend Hannah, you'll remember to "take the vitamins" and "count the ravens."

VALERIE WOERNER, owner and creator of Val Marie Paper prayer journals and author of *Grumpy Mom Takes a Holiday*

Focus is a secret sauce for success. In this entertaining book, Hannah Brencher becomes your personal coach and mentor to help you address your inner critic, gain focus, and achieve your dreams. If you're looking to accomplish that next big thing in your life, this book is for you!

PROMISE TANGEMAN, founder and art director, GoLive

Someone with as much talent as Hannah Brencher has, a true modern-day wordsmith, could easily stay at a safe distance on the sure, solid ground of pedestals and stages. But Hannah knows that lives never get changed from safe distances and our true purpose is never found in the applause. So she comes down from those shiny stages and bright lights, looks you straight in the eye, and tells you, "We can't stay here. It's time to leave these dark woods behind." Hannah's words become not just a fight song, but a lifeline to everyone who needs it. It's a survival guide, an anthem, a new way in the wilderness. You *need* this book in your life!

MARY MARANTZ, bestselling author of *Dirt* and host of The Mary Marantz Show

fighting forward

Your NITTY-GRITTY GUIDE to BEATING the LIES that HOLD YOU BACK

HANNAH BRENCHER

ZONDERVAN
BOOKS

ZONDERVAN BOOKS

Fighting Forward
Copyright © 2021 by Hannah Brencher

Requests for information should be addressed to:
Zondervan, *3900 Sparks Dr. SE, Grand Rapids, Michigan 49546*

Zondervan titles may be purchased in bulk for educational, business, fundraising, or sales promotional use. For information, please email SpecialMarkets@Zondervan.com.

ISBN 978-0-310-35086-6 (softcover)
ISBN 978-0-310-35090-3 (ebook)

The author is represented by Mackenzie Brady Watson of Stuart Krichevsky Literary Agency.

Cover design: Connie Gabbert
Interior design: Kait Lamphere

Printed in the United States of America

20 21 22 23 24 25 26 27 28 29 30 /LSC/ 15 14 13 12 11 10 9 8 7 6 5 4 3 2 1

To my Novi girl—
every word in this book
was written with you in mind.
Keep fighting forward
into every good and glorious thing
that God has for you.

Contents

Foreword by Shelley Giglio..............................xi

The Method.. xv

PART 1: Get Ready, Get Set

1. Just Show Up 3
2. Rebuild on the Ruins 11
3. Switch the Script 17

PART 2: Go

4. Commit to Mile One............................. 29
5. Take the Vitamins............................... 37
6. Lay the Bricks.................................. 43
7. Say Yes to Slow Magic.......................... 50
8. Put Your Blinders On 56
9. Promise Me You'll Fail 62
10. Watch for Foxes 71

PART 3: Roadblocks + Plateaus

11. Go into the Darkroom 79
12. Count the Ravens.............................. 86

13. Lay Down the Arrows.......................... 93

14. Evict the Envy 98

15. Stand Still 104

16. Give Up the Ghosts........................... 110

17. Step Out of the Woods 116

PART 4: Cheerleaders

18. Make the Sign................................. 123

19. Hold Me in the Light.......................... 131

20. Walk Me through the Rain 138

PART 5: Steady Paces + Finish Lines

21. Look How Far We've Come..................... 145

22. Step Back in Love............................. 153

23. Fight for Rest 161

24. Build the Fire 169

25. Go Find Sarah 176

26. Finish Well 182

27. Operate from the Overflow 188

Fight Forward: A Final Song for You 195

Acknowledgments 199

Notes 203

Foreword

Hannah Brencher—I don't know many people like her. I honestly don't know if many like her exist. Her love for life and people is just flat-out astonishing. When I first heard Hannah's name, people were just coming to know and understand her heart. She had written *If You Find This Letter*—which you should also read—and the friends I knew who were talking endlessly about her were in awe. The conversations centered around, "How does a person take on the needs/prayers/care of a whole city?" Hannah was showing us that to do so, we must love one beautiful person at a time.

Hannah did just that. As a way of working through some of her own struggles for significance and value, she decided to focus on someone other than herself. She decided, not just for her own healing but definitely as a part of it, to care for someone else who was also finding themselves in desperate need of love.

Today, as Hannah lives in my city and worships in my community, I continue to see this choice of attitude and heart. She is convinced that even if she can't personally love everyone, she will never be dismissed from loving someone, and loving them well. She inspires me every day.

In this book, Hannah again shows up to her life and message and calling. This artistic work consistently shows her willingness to forgo the shortcuts of self-preservation and to encourage us to fight with resilience and consistency in the battle against settling for less, thus creating the desire and strength to believe for more. Hannah has taught me more about discipline and daily rhythms of health and growth than any other person I'm around. She is committed to teaching us what she's learned. This isn't pie-in-the-sky talk, a theory of what might work; this is a well-worn path she has traveled down through many ups and downs and is willing to share as a help to us. And share she does. The principles and foundations expressed will shape us for the rest of our lives.

This is the kind of book that will have you taking daily notes and tacking them to every surface you see as a reminder of the promise and hope extended over your life. It's the kind of offering you'll read again and again to remind you that you may make mistakes, but instead of those defining you, they'll stretch the muscles that make you grow into someone of immense beauty and strength. That some of the things that seem hardest to endure in life end up giving you a platform of understanding and grace you can extend to others in the same places.

When I think about our future, I can't help but consider the opportunity before us. As one who is officially ahead of many of you in years, I can't help but dream with you about all that God will do in and through your life. God promises that the purposes he has for our lives will be fulfilled (Proverbs 19:21). I've now lived long enough to have experienced some of that promise. I think it seems safer in our culture to just believe God for less in case less is what he can do. It's also more plausible to think he would have trouble using our messed-up lives than it is to believe he can redeem them and repurpose them in a world full of hurt and need. Watching Hannah's life and story makes me believe again that he has big plans for you. Today, as you begin to read this book, I pray that hope and courage will find you. I pray that your eyes will be opened to the promise of God, not just for the whole world, but for *you*. I pray that you will know our God is big enough, strong enough, and in control enough to take the things we have done, and the things done to us, and redeem them and use them for a higher purpose and greater calling. Ask him for that today. Call on his name, the one great name, and ask him to reveal day by day his stunning path for you. Nothing would make Hannah prouder than to see you take your place in this hurting world with a life saved and called for such a time as this.

Read on in peace today. God has words just for you: *fighting forward*.

Your fellow journeyer,

Shelley Giglio, cofounder of Passion
Conferences and Passion City Church

The Method

In this very moment, there's someone trying to hold you back.

They're strong and persistent, and they'd whisper nearly anything in your ear right about now to keep you from turning the page or showing up to that event later or finally believing you have what it takes to go after that dream of yours.

They're crafty and cunning, planting little seeds of doubt within your story line, delighting when you start telling yourself things like, "I don't deserve better than this" or "I'll never measure up" or "I don't have what it takes."

Fear—the name I've come to give it over years of spending time with it—thrives off of your playing small and repeating anthems of helplessness to yourself. If it can get you to believe seemingly harmless lies about yourself, it can go in for the bigger stuff. It can set up camp in your brain and allow all its liar minions to take over how you think and how you step out into this world.

The truth is, what you have to offer this world is far too good and far too necessary for you to accept these heartless anthems that Fear sings into you. And what Fear doesn't want you to know is that you're capable of stringing together better ballads, ones that don't just help you fight back against the lie but help you fight forward into all the better things waiting for you up ahead.

I'm not sure if you've ever heard of a "fight song" before, but this book is full of them.

I started writing fight songs several years ago when I was experiencing the lowest point of my life. Diagnosed with severe depression and waiting on answers from God and doctors, I wrote journal entries at the time that were a grand display of just how much fear and anxiety I was drowning in—thoughts that I would never add up, that I would never be free, that I would always be in this pit.

And then, out of nowhere, I remember this brief blip of hope that the darkness would not win and I would come out of this. I grabbed tightly to that hope—the hope that I would walk differently and be even better one day for having gone through this.

On Christmas Eve of that year in the dark, I drove to the local convenience store just a half mile from my house and bought a black composition notebook. I went home, pulled a silver Sharpie from the cupboard, and wrote the words "FIGHT SONG" on the binding of the notebook.

I honestly can't claim to know where the idea came from, apart from someone who sent me an email with a link to a song telling me she had a hunch I might need these words.

I didn't know the girl and she didn't know the darkness I was in, but I think she saved my life.

I remember sitting at my computer after clicking into that link and listening for the very first time to "Fight Song" by Rachel Platten. And something clicked in my brain as I heard this ballad about a young woman who was choosing not to give up but rather to fight forward in the face of fear.

I refer to the moments when I encountered hope and belief that I would one day walk out of these woods as breadcrumbs. Yes, like the story of Hansel and Gretel, where the two children were instructed to litter the ground with breadcrumbs so they'd find a way to get back home if they ever became lost in the woods.

This song was the first breadcrumb of many to come.

In that black composition notebook, I began to tell a different story. They weren't songs, per se, because I'm a storyteller with a hopeless addiction to prose. They were the start of a collection of stronger words. More hopeful words. I thought that maybe one day I'd have a child, and that child would be roaming around the house on a boring, rainy afternoon looking for something to do when they'd stumble upon this journal at the back of the bookshelf, just as I encountered my mother's journals from young adulthood and read them all.

I knew that if I ever had a child who would come across this notebook, I would want them to know that they too are capable of fighting forward when the darkness tries to win. I would want to tell them to be strong and to not be afraid. I would want them to know they are already good enough, that they do not need to fling their life away to a culture that tells them to modify and edit themselves in order to belong. More than anything, I would want them to know that you can fight your way back to yourself, find your way home, even when fear tries to dictate a story to you about always standing in one place. You could come out of the woods. You could help others do the same. You could keep on living when it would be easier to give up.

Each word and every sentence you encounter here has been marinated in the hope that you will pick up your bags and keep moving forward, away from the fear that wants to convince you to live small. That you won't allow anxiety or insecurity to stop you from moving into beautiful territories. That you will borrow these words when you need truth and you will pass them forward like a baton in a race when someone else needs them more.

I wish I could fill this space with all the customized solutions you need to change your life or find your ultimate purpose. I could draw you the map I followed and then pass it to you.

But your map is different because you're the one who needs to draw it.

What I can do, what I've always loved to do, is stand by the roadside with a glittering sign that reads in big letters, "YOU'VE GOT THIS!" as you run on by me.

What I can do is write fight songs in the night for you, during the hours when I encountered fear in its most crippling state, and remind you to keep putting one foot in front of the other.

These are the reminders, on the days when you don't even know you need a reminder, that you're already operating from a space of worthiness. God already looks at you and thinks you're enough. Even if you never did another impressive thing in this lifetime, he would still want to tell all the angels about you.

This might very well be the fight for your life, as it was my own, the fight to take back all that fear tried to steal from you. This might be the dinner bell going off in the distance, calling you to wake up and stop living life like a ghost—afraid to be seen or to take up too much space.

It's going so fast, and you're going to miss every little mile marker if you're stuck inside your head with an inner critical troll who tells you you're no good. You will miss out on all of it—the joy you could have had, the memories you could have made, the life that passed you by like an elevator that stopped at your floor but you didn't get in before the doors closed.

It's time to move.

It's time to leave this place behind.

Part 1

GET READY, GET SET

Perfection is not the goal; consistency is. All of life is the showing up to try to be steadfast toward what we love—God, people, causes.

You're never too _____ to begin again.

Chapter 1

Just Show Up

It may be time for you to just start. To not waste any more moments. To not wait on perfection. But to just get up from the floor, with wobbly knees, and start moving imperfectly into that thing that fear is always trying to hold you back from.

I can't even begin to count the number of people I meet who have a goal, a vision of who they want to become, that they never move toward because they're too afraid of failing. They're afraid of what people will think. They're afraid of not being successful in the end and inevitably breaking their own heart. The thing is, more hearts break every day over never taking that first step than anything else.

I think most of us feel this fear. Somewhere in our younger years, we learned to carry this expectation that we'd be exceptional. We'd be good. We'd do all the right things. We'd be perfect.

Maybe you learned to tell yourself, *If perfection isn't a realistic expectation, I will just get as close to perfect as possible.* And these words you spoke over yourself cracked open the back door just wide enough for fear to get in. Soon enough, you became someone who writes but never presses publish. Or someone who buys the running shoes but never takes the first run. A person who always wanted to paint but never picked up the brush. Or the one who wanted to go back to school but whose internal dialogue prevented them from ever filling out the application.

This is what fear will do if we opt for perfection over choosing to start just as we are in this moment.

There are no shortcuts. There are no overnight fixes. There are no detours. The instruction manual for deep change is the same every single day: *Show up. Show up. Show up.*

You've probably heard that phrase a bunch. People say it all the time. But this isn't a call for you to show up when things are easy and convenient. If you wait on convenience, the time will likely never be right. There's no way to cut corners on the hard parts of life that really help to form the person you're becoming. Trust me, you don't want to skip those parts, as hard as they will be to endure. The tough conversations. The endless goodbye. The "thank you" she never extended in your direction. The way it sounded when the front door closed and you knew it was really, definitely over.

These things likely would have never happened if you hadn't shown up. And sometimes they'll hurt so bad you'll be tempted to not show up again, to keep your heart locked up inside a safe where only you know the combination. But you'll miss so much if you live that way.

Even if life breaks your heart, decide to show up anyway, because the scars are worth the purpose you fought for. They're proof you were here. They're proof you struggled and you believed in something. They're proof you laced up your shoes and entered the game with your whole heart.

I read a book recently titled *Atomic Habits* in the hope it would change everything about my life. That's just how I operate. I believe I am always a thirty-day plan away from a completely new landscape. I'm a transformation junkie, and I have no hopes of recovering.

The book did change some things though. My favorite story was about a man who decided he wanted to take back his life and lose weight. He began going to the gym every single day.[1]

But that's just it.

That's all he did for the first few months.

He would walk inside the gym, put on his gear, and sit in the gym. That was the only promise he made to himself: "I'm going to show up to this gym and at least sit here for the next five minutes." For the first month, he didn't allow himself to do anything else.

Day after day, the method repeated itself until he felt ready to stay a little longer and inch a little bit further outside his comfort zone.

Some may think it's ineffective and pointless to even drive to the gym, sit on a bench for a few minutes, and head back home. But I know the feeling, and you probably do too, of making a promise to yourself that you could not keep. It's not because the promise was bad—whether it was to eat healthier or write the book or go back to school. Sometimes the promise is just too unrealistic for where you're currently at. It must be broken up into bits. And the first bit is always *showing up*.

Showing up to sit on a bench in a gym.

Showing up to read the first sentence.

Showing up to eat one leaf of kale.

Showing up to fill out the first line of an application.

This slow progress could change the world. Turns out, it often does.

The opposite of showing up is opting out.

Sometimes I deal with anxiety when it comes to social situations, and my first instinct is not to show up at all. I think the culture has made it really comfortable to claim you want a lazy night on the couch away from others because then you won't have to have deep conversations or endure small talk or commit to more things. It's a sour-grapes attitude, and I am really trying to work on it.

My husband, Lane, keeps reminding me to change the way I'm talking about events on the calendar, and I've started opening up to others about it, admitting that I've created a problem where there wasn't one before. That I have all these things on my calendar, and I treat them like hurdles to get over rather than opportunities that God may want me to step into. I do a really bad job of being present for other people when I don't even feel like being in the moment.

I have one friend whom I always text when I don't feel like going somewhere. I fill the space with all my reasons that it doesn't matter if I don't go. I want her to be swayed and tell me to stay home and just enjoy my me time. But she always replies, "Yeah, the things you don't want to go to end up being the best for you." That's it.

And she's always right. When I feel resistance, it means something is about to happen.

So I've been switching up my prayers these days. I've been making them compact but honest. I've been straight-out telling God, "I'm afraid I won't add up in this place. Help wipe out this fear and see what you need me to see instead." It's a good prayer. It's working. But I have to pray it all the time. For me, it's not a onetime prayer but a ballad I keep reciting to God every time I encounter a new hurdle.

I lived for too long believing that showing up was ineffective if I was still afraid. The fear may still linger, but there is power in ignoring the fear and taking that first step anyway.

When in spite of your fear you choose to go after the things that matter to you, you're actively saying to the fear, "I know you want to try to hold me back from this, but I am going to show up, no matter what. So you can go and pick a better subject, but I won't be subdued by your efforts anymore."

When you start showing up, you learn that some of the most beautiful things only happened because you found the courage to exit your own head and just do the next necessary thing.

This was the essential lesson I learned when I pushed my fears aside and just slapped a smile on my face for the occasions coming up on my calendar. When I stopped going to the grocery store with headphones in my ears, trying to tune out other people. When I became open to the things God wanted to do with my day instead of scheduling so tightly that nothing miraculous or wonder-filled could get in.

Sometimes you show up, and you keep showing up, because of someone else. Someone who needs you and what you bring to the table. Someone who looks at you and at how far you've come and says, "I want to be like that." Consistency is like espresso down the hall: it comes with an aroma that other people can sense and will gravitate toward. I've learned that if I am going to be any kind of person by the end of my life, I want to be the consistent kind.

You'll start seeing shifts in tiny ways. You may be tempted to discount the movements because the change will be so small, but don't move so quickly. Step back. Jot down the small "showing up" miracle.

I was in the grocery store just the other day, getting groceries for the week. I was picking out some hummus, and a woman came alongside me and asked, "Why should I eat this?"

"Excuse me?" I was caught off guard by her question.

"Why should I eat this?" she said again. "And how? With crackers?"

"I like it with crackers," I tell her. "Or carrots. I love to dip my carrots in hummus."

"Hmm," she said to me. "That's a good idea."

A few minutes later she was alongside me again as I went through the cheese aisle.

"What's that?" she asked me, pointing to the little log of cheese in my hand.

"It's goat cheese," I tell her. "With little berries in it."

"Oh!" she exclaimed. "Now I like that! Which one should I get?"

She proceeded to tell me she had gone to the doctor recently, and he had advised her to start eating better. The problem was she didn't have any experiences to go off of; she didn't know the first thing about eating healthy, and the doctor hadn't really equipped her.

She just arrived in the parking lot of the grocery store, went in, grabbed a basket, and showed up with anticipation. And there I was. A woman who usually has her headphones in but didn't that day.

I started showing her what was in my basket and what I loved to eat on a daily basis. I watched as her face glowed with new ideas—how happy she was to encounter someone who didn't dread vegetables.

The exchange was small and almost insignificant, but I know it helped her. I know it made her more confident in those new changes she was making.

You never know when you're showing up somewhere because someone else needs you. Because they have questions. Because they walked into that day unsure of how it would unfold. This is the beautiful part of life—we need one another to make it all the way through the story.

I think there is such power in showing up, even when you're not sure about what you offer or whether you can make an impact. My husband, Lane, is a part of the student ministry at our church. He leads a pack of ninth-grade boys, which I can bet is not an easy age group when it comes to trying to get them to open up and share their feelings. When he made this commitment, he was nervous. Unsure of himself. Unsure of what he had to offer. They'd all been meeting up for a long time, and he was the new one in the group. I can only imagine how hard it is to walk into a group that has already formed a strong bond and insert yourself. Yet he's been showing up for the last six months.

At the moment of this writing, Lane is somewhere in South Carolina in a minivan packed with those ninth-grade boys on his way to a Weezer concert. The concert doesn't start until 8:00 p.m., and he likely won't get back to Atlanta until two or three in the morning. Everything he's experiencing right now sounds like my personal nightmare, but I can't tell you how proud I am of him for driving the minivan, for taking those boys through the McDonald's drive-through at one in the morning.

We grabbed breakfast before he left for the trip, and he opened up to me about how there was a time when the boys didn't even acknowledge him. How it wasn't until he spent a weekend with them that he felt like they knew him or wanted to be around him. We talked about how one day, if not this day, it was going to mean something big to them that he was one of those consistent forces in their lives. That they would never forget that one time they got the chance to pile into a minivan to travel one state over to see a band in concert. You don't forget those experiences. They become a part of your growing up.

"People remember people who stay," I told him.

I think we all remember the people in our lives who were consistent with us. That's one of the cool side effects of showing up, no matter the cost. Because eventually, when you get so good at the showing up, you become a person who stayed. And that will mean so much to someone one day.

All the good love stories have only ever happened in this world because two people stayed.

All the good friendships have only ever withstood the tough seasons because two people stayed.

All the inspiring transformations have only ever stayed in the "after" instead of slipping back into the "before" because someone stayed.

They became fluent in the art of showing up.

It won't always be easy. And you may go through times when you feel like you're the only one who shows up consistently. Keep flexing that muscle. Out of consistency grows trust. Out of trust grows loyalty. Out of loyalty comes the steady ordinary. You may not see it right now, but the ordinary is the gold of this lifetime.

Before we move forward, you need to know this truth: You are not alone. You—at the starting line or picking up where you left off years ago—are not alone. It's tempting to believe everyone else has it all together and is moving forward with no difficulty at all, but we're all overcoming hurdles and roadblocks in our own ways. You are surrounded, even if you don't see it. You are capable of showing up to the things that are right in front of you today.

So here's to first steps.

To lacing up the shoes and taking that first run.

To sending the text or writing that first paragraph.

To filling out the application or saying that first prayer.

You don't have to see the whole story of how things will unfold outlined in front of you. It's much simpler than that. Just decide to show up to this day—this very hour—with everything you have. And then repeat the same thing tomorrow. You never know how close to the breakthrough you actually are. Don't quit before the miracles start to happen.

Chapter 2

Rebuild on the Ruins

"You don't know how to show up for people. You don't know how to truly, truly be there for them in a time of need."

This was the subtle but loud voice of fear that clanked around on the inside of me all throughout 2017. It was this fear that put me in a headlock and really sent me into a stretch of time when I didn't feel God.

Every time the fear showed up, I bowed to it. I fixed it a plate. I gave it a bed. I entertained it. And the fear didn't just go away or go off to find another victim; it sucked out all my confidence. It caused me to believe I didn't deserve good things. I stopped opening myself up to others. I doubted every word that came out of my mouth. I adopted an eggshell lifestyle.

An eggshell lifestyle is the kind of life you live when you're afraid to make a mistake or get it wrong. It's like that ditty, "Step on a crack, you'll break your mother's back." We get so cautious and fearful of the cracks in our own stories that the only thing we end up breaking is ourselves.

The catalyst to this fear was losing a friend. I honestly didn't know that losing a friend would hurt so much, that I would spend many days waking up as if someone had just ripped vital organs out of me. I guess I naively thought you just reach a point where you don't lose friends anymore. That's what I thought a huge chunk of adulthood was—finding friends who really lasted forever.

Turns out, you can absolutely lose the person you were used to calling when everything felt like it was falling apart.

The thing no one ever taught me about losing a friend is how closely it mirrors romantic heartbreak.

I went through all the motions of a breakup. I cried. I became angry. I was desperate and bitter. I said things I didn't mean. I stalked them on social media. I wallowed. I felt like all the prayers I was sending to God were coming back with a big "RETURN TO SENDER" label stamped on the outside of me.

When I reached the end of 2017, I fell into the trap I think a lot of us fall into. I believed the turning of the page to a new year was going to erase all the pain from the story. I thought to myself, *I can rebuild. I can get stronger. I can move out of this space on the map where I don't want to be.*

I became the spokesperson for the end of 2017. I was the girl with a gown and a crown on, waving goodbye to 2017 while sitting on top of the convertible in the parade.

I think this why people love the prospect of a new year. There's the hope—if only for a brief moment—that we can walk away from whatever held us back the year before and declare that this is the year when everything changes. All of it. This will be the year we lose the weight. This will be the year we eat all the kale and read all the books and have the spiritual capacity of a monk. This will be the year when no hard stuff happens. When life is good and blessed and free of pain.

It's only in adulthood that I've learned the good usually comes with the hard. The good and the hard are mixed together like Funfetti into the cake. We can't really separate the two.

I saw 2018 emerging out of the murky waters, and I was ready to go running for it. I was full-on sprinting into the new year when God grabbed me by the collar of my sweatshirt and yanked me back with a fierce tenderness, as if to say, "You need to stop. Before you move any farther, I need you to stop. You see something you want to get rid of, wipe off the map, and I see something that was necessary. Don't you see it? I use the hard stuff all the time. Don't discount the brokenness—I am using it to bring you to some of the best parts of the story."

I hate to bring the bad news, but a clock striking midnight on December 31 won't change your circumstances. It may give you a sweet dopamine release and a belief in yourself for the next forty-eight hours, but it won't necessarily mean everything will be different when you arrive in a new year.

Just because a new calendar shows up doesn't mean the things that hurt you last year won't come back around this year. A resolution won't cover whatever broke last year—it will still be there, and it will still quite likely demand to be felt.

At the beginning of a new year, I usually pick a word I want to represent the twelve months ahead. It's become a more meaningful practice to me than setting goals.

I've had all kinds of words in the last few years: *Strong. Home. Joy. Freedom.* But on this particular year, I found myself reading the book of Jeremiah in the Bible when I came across a line that surprised me:

"The city will be rebuilt on her ruins."

Just that line. I'd never noticed it before.

That line comes up in verse 18 of chapter 30 in Jeremiah's book. To know the writer Jeremiah is to know that God downloaded a lot of good stuff into his heart so he could go and tell others. He was a prophet. He saw things before they happened.

At this point in the story, Jeremiah was giving the Israelites some hope that there would be healing and rebuilding in their land after a long stretch of ruins. He was declaring that every level of society would be renewed in the coming days, that people would live in towns built on mounds of rubble.

This is where I have to pause and scratch my head. Like, *Did you really mean to do this, God? Did you really mean to rebuild on top of a mess?* This is not what I think happens to the ruins in my own story. I do not look at the ugly mounds or pieces of scrap metal and see something to build on. I see something worth hiding away and covering up. But to know God is to know he wants your best. Day after day, he wants the most unscripted and unedited version of you. He can always work with that.

Even though I believe this statement exactly 82 percent of the time, I am still the one who tries frantically to clear the junk away on my own. Like, if God were making house visits, I would be the one piling all the ugly unseen junk into the upstairs closet, thinking to myself, *It will be safe and concealed here.*

I picture God strolling into the house and taking a look around. He doesn't admire what I want him to admire. He doesn't survey the sturdiness of the IKEA barstools or drool over the chandelier. He simply says, "Can I see the closet?"

I protest. I start to freak out. I panic, thinking, *You cannot handle my mess, the things I've hidden there.*

But God in his character is kind and calm as he tells me, "What I will not do is discount your ruins. I want all of you—even the stuff you hid in the guest bedroom closet. I am not throwing away the parts of your story that left you feeling crumbled and defeated. You don't have to hide those parts. Let's use them."

And with that, God does exactly what that verse in Jeremiah says. He rebuilds a city on top of what once ruined us.

There are going to be broken times when you feel as if everything is under demolition. When things feel unresolved or ruined inside of you. When the only thing you might have the strength to do is three-quarters-of-the-way trust that God will take the broken pieces and glue them back together.

That's called *kintsugi*.

Kintsugi is a Japanese term that means "join with gold" or "golden seams." If you were to break a jar and wanted to put it back together using the method of *kintsugi*, someone would take the jar and piece it back together with a glue that is mixed with powdered gold or platinum. It wouldn't be like superglue, where the item looks perfect because the glue is clear. You would see the gold in all the cracks. You would know that the object has breaks in it.

Those who practice *kintsugi* believe that just because something breaks doesn't mean it cannot be used anymore. It's not about perfection; it's about resilience. The once broken thing becomes more valuable because now there is gold binding the pieces together. As author J. K. Rowling once told a Harvard University graduating class, "The knowledge that you have emerged wiser and stronger from setbacks means that you are, ever after, secure in your ability to survive."[2]

Now you have golden seams holding all the parts of you together and making you stronger for whatever is coming next.

So maybe you and I need a better song to sing in the moments when the low feels too low to pinpoint on a map, because it's not about your fingers hovering over the Delete button when the mess comes.

Maybe we are meant to look back on those hard things and find the golden seams in them. To discover how they prepared us. How they grew us up. How they changed us. How they made us strong. How they made us believe that every last ruin in our story could be used to rebuild a city one day.

The "new year, new you" never happens overnight at the

stroke of twelve. But it can happen brick by brick as we trust God to rebuild our ruins.

Because here's the truth: God uses all the pieces. Every little thing. Nothing is wasted. Even when he builds the new in us, he is reaching back to use the old. A few months ago, I was digging deep into Isaiah 43:19—the part where God leans in and says, "Don't look back. I'm doing a new thing." The phrase "new thing" in the Hebrew is *chadash*. It means fresh and new (not surprisingly). But if you look even closer, you will learn that the root of this word means "to rebuild, renew, repair." The prefix *re* means "again and again and again." So God is saying to us, "I'm not discounting what you've walked through. I am using the stories you swore would discount you, and I am piecing them together to bring you to something new."

Over the parts of our stories we want to white out or forget for good, God says, "Hey, I see what you've been through. I'm renewing that. I'm renewing you. Again and again and again. I am taking all the broken pieces and rebuilding you on what you thought would destroy you."

Chapter 3

Switch the Script

Earlier this year, I decided to name my inner critic. At this point in my life, I am well aware of the critic and his games. His methods of keeping me standing one place, never putting myself out there, are tired and old. I am sick of them. So I figured that to approach this voice in my brain taunting me with anthems of "not good enough," I needed to give him a proper name; otherwise he'd be just an ethereal feeling floating in the air. I am a believer that giving something a name breaks some of its power. I'm all for breaking the power of my inner critic.

I settled on the name Sid after the scrawny bully in *Toy Story* who wears a skull T-shirt at all times and wreaks havoc for all the toys in the neighborhood. Now it is so much easier to address Sid because I know his name.

I can say, "Sid, shut up" or "Sid, be quiet." I can recognize that this unkind and often annoying critic in my brain is not speaking out of love, and I can put it in its place.

I wrote an essay recently about Sid in which I challenged anyone reading to give their inner critic a good, solid name. The response was so overwhelming that I think there should be a national holiday for naming our inner critics.

This is what amazed me when people wrote back to introduce me to their inner critic—so many chose to name their inner critics after real people who had hurt them or discounted them or antagonized them along the way.

A young woman named Hannah decided to name her inner critic Heather because when someone got her name wrong, they almost always called her Heather instead. This was the perfect name for her inner critic because her critic always rattled on about how she wasn't seen and wasn't truly known. Being called the wrong name reinforced this fear that she wasn't known.

Another woman, Jennifer, named her inner critic Lois. Lois had perfect hair, perfect lipstick, and impeccable timing. She showed up just as Jennifer was taking pizza rolls out of the oven for her children and then again when Jennifer pulled out the dry shampoo and left yesterday's makeup intact when getting ready for the day. Lois has a lot to say about progress and assures Jennifer that slow progress isn't progress at all.

I've learned that Sid isn't a truth teller. He's quite the unreliable narrator. He's not the kind of person you should trust or get in the car with. He's like a tour guide with no real knowledge of the area. He's just spitting out loads of words and hoping I will accept them as fact. If Sid has his way, he will convince me to compromise my day, my dreams, my visions, and the beauty of my life. He will choke it out. With a name like Sid, he seems harmless, but that's the first mistake we make—thinking the little lies can't hurt us if we give them just enough space to breathe.

The little lies add up. They're more powerful and toxic than you think.

A couple of years ago, Lane and I signed up for a community service project. On a cold, rainy Saturday morning in February, we showed up at a park to spend a few hours cleaning it up. I was confused when we got there because to me it looked like a park: grass, mud, trees, and brush. But I couldn't see anything we might need to "do" to improve this park.

We trudged through the mud to the back of the park with our group, carrying shovels and clippers and trash bags. The man at the front of the pack explained to us that we were going to spend the morning cutting down invasive plants. I remember looking around the woods and thinking to myself, *Where are all the invasive plants? How are we going to know how to do this?*

The man began to point out these weird vinelike plants that were rooted in the ground but made their way up the trees we were standing under. I would have told you this was just a part of it—that these crazy threadlike vines were just part of the nature surrounding us. Turns out, these were the invasive plants known as kudzu, and if we did not cut them and uproot them, they would eventually kill the trees around us.

This was crazy to me. The vines were so small, and the trees around them were pillars; they were giants compared to the vines. I was so shocked that something that looked so harmless could be such a deadly killer.

With a few essential instructions, we went to work cutting out the invasive plants that were spreading from the ground and up through the trees, wrapping themselves tightly around the trunks. We learned it wasn't enough to simply cut the invasive plant. First, we needed to release the tree from the grip of the plant. Then we needed to figure out where the root of the invasive plant was and dig up the root. After we dug up the root and threw it into a pile, we had to spray the ends to make sure the plant wouldn't keep spreading. It was quite an extensive process.

I usually never get emotional over nature. Where my mom finds God in a sunset or on a beach, I've always been one of those people who does not really connect with God through nature.

I like to find him in books and sentences, in people and stories. But that day, with a shovel and spray bottle in hand, I saw God in the process of uprooting the invasives. I found myself tearing up as I cut the plants off the trees, only to find that the plants had done their worst. There were deep indentations in the trunks of those trees—scars that would be there for a long time—that made me realize how deeply the invasives cut into something meant to spread beauty and bring life to the forest around it.

I don't think anything in life is accidental, so it wasn't a coincidence that Lane and I were charged with this job. At that point, we had hit the one-year married mark, but I was struggling daily. My thoughts were a mess. I was going through the motions and letting each tiny feeling push me over and dictate my days. I'd reached a point where I thought, *Maybe this is just who I am. Maybe I am one of those people who will experience little joy and happiness, and I should just become okay with that.* Lane felt completely helpless to make me better. He was constantly affirming me and building me up, but it wasn't until that day in the woods that I realized I'd let the simple lies take too much root. I'd let them suffocate me and steal so much joy from me. I was listening to voices in my brain telling me on repeat that I was never going to be happy, never going to feel joy, and never be free. And I wish I could tell you that I didn't believe them, but I absolutely did.

I silently cried as we worked to free these trees, thinking about how many of the lies I let come in without a fight. I could see a collection of them in my brain, choking the life out of me—out of my thoughts, my visions, and my plans. It was time to fight harder. It was time to uproot the lies. It was time to dig into a better truth.

There's a verse in the Psalms that I've heard nearly a hundred times without giving it a second thought: "You anoint my head with oil; my cup overflows."[3]

That line—*you anoint my head with oil*—makes me think of a picture of someone sitting in a seat while someone else pours a basin of oil over them, a practice I don't understand. When you don't understand, there is God and Google to take you a level deeper in your faith.

"You anoint my head with oil" is a reference to a shepherd who pours oil over the heads of his sheep through a practice called "backlining." Daily, sheep have oil poured over their heads and down their backs to protect them from a seemingly harmless enemy—the blowfly. The blowfly is known to fly up the sheep's nose and plant eggs in its brain. The sheep will become so irritated by the fly that it will bang its head against the ground to try to get it out. They can die from trying to relieve the irritation. Thanks to the oil on the head, the flies will slide out instead of flying in.

Here I was thinking anointing the head with oil was a super holy process used on royalty when it's really a practical, daily method to keep the minds of the sheep right. And the psalmist says this is what God does for us daily. He pours oils over us so our brains are protected. God has never been unaware that our minds can be crazy and dark.

In her book *Operating Instructions*, Anne Lamott quotes "this guy I know" as saying, "My mind is a bad neighborhood that I try not to go into alone."[4] I feel this on a deep and spiritual level. Until these last few years, I never understood the importance of maintaining my mind or checking for the scripts I am believing or cutting out the lies. I had to wake up and realize I would have to fight for a healthier brain, and that God joins me in that fight every single day.

But the "anointing the head with oil" thing—what does that look like practically for someone with a mind overrun by hoodlums of fear? What is the "how" in that daily practice? I'm a peddler of practicality when it comes to growing our faith, so I'll just tell you a few things that worked well for me to uproot the lies and find a better anthem.

Replace lies with truth. Whenever I feel anxious or overcome by lies, I engage in a simple practice. I pull out a sheet of paper and write down every lie I am tempted to believe at that moment. The big ones. The small ones. The ugly ones. The hilarious ones. When those lies are sitting on the page, I don't come back at myself with affirmations, but I go to the place I've always gone to find the truth: the Word of God.

I will spend some time looking up passages that directly combat the lie I am tempted to believe. Sometimes I will bring the lie out into the light and ask God to show me where it started or to give me a better alternative. It can feel like an arduous task sometimes, but the work is worth it. Little by little and lie by lie, I start to believe a better story for myself. I start to feel freer.

I made my friend Brooke do this with me one day. We ended up lighting candles, playing moody music, and speaking our lies out loud. It was pretty powerful to engage in the process with someone else who knows me well. She and I were able to speak up and say to one another, "That lie is absolutely ridiculous. I know you, and I know you are good and you are kind and you get better every single day."

Give grace-filled pep talks to yourself. I have a great capacity to say unkind things to myself and call myself all sorts of bad names. But I am working on grace and on trying to understand that I am a gatekeeper for my mind and heart and so I have to use better words when talking to myself and it's okay to expect better things for my life. If I would not think to use these words on a friend, I am definitely not going to use them on myself.

I started a practice of giving myself grace-filled pep talks years ago, but I've ramped it up in recent times. Before I lived in Atlanta, I lived in Connecticut. The town where I lived had the inconvenient problem of no airports nearby, and I was traveling every week. So every week, I'd wake up at the crack of dawn, throw my luggage in the car in a "I don't need no man" fashion, drive an hour to the airport, park in some obscure lot, shuttle to the airport, get through security, hop on the first flight—and (without question) always need to hop on a second or third flight because the airport in Connecticut has very few direct flights— and get to my destination to turn around and reverse the process the very next day.

I was just twenty-three years old and already aging myself by ten years every time I geared up for another excursion. Add to this that flying on an airplane always comes with its fair share of problems—the airplane is always late or the flight is canceled for no apparent reason or they're missing a flight attendant and the replacement is forty minutes from the airport.

The problems are endless, and the only way I figured out how to fight the steps that aged me was by learning to coach myself through the steps. I would say, *Okay, babycakes, get up at the crack of dawn; Okay, girl, you've made it to the airport; you've got this next step;* or *Hey, babe, you have time to spare, so go get yourself some nuggets.* Instead of hating the twelve-step airport process, I coached myself through every step with kind words and kind names.

Ask for the truth. If you surround yourself with truth tellers, then at any given moment, they can swat the flies for you and tell you the truth. On days when fear is having a field day with my thoughts, I ask Lane questions about the fear. "Is this true? Is this accurate? Could this be something I need to pay attention to?" Most of the time the answer is, "No, it's not true; it's an irrational thought," but it helps to hear that from someone who has your best interests in mind.

When the lies are thick, it's best to not accept them as truth and to turn to reliable people in your life who can give you the real truth and point you back to God. If you don't have reliable people to tell you anything good, then download an app on your phone where you can listen to the Bible. I'm not kidding about this. The psalms are a great place to start listening because they're a perfect blend of reality. The psalms don't shy away from the chaos, but they always end with hope. If your inner critic has nothing nice or kind to say to you, turn on your Bible and let the sweet British narrator speak better words over your life.

Preach to yourself. In Psalm 42, we read about a person who's in great distress. He is crying out to God, and the words of his song are anguished and raw. I encounter such hope when I read this psalm because it reminds me that we always have permission to be honest before God, that he doesn't need me to sugarcoat things. He wants me in my most real state.

At one point, the psalmist asks himself, "Hey, soul, why are you so down in the dumps? What's going on inside of you?" I love this part. It took me years to realize that the writer of this psalm is speaking directly to himself. He is questioning what is going on inside of him. He is realizing that this dark, thick doubt isn't God, and he is speaking boldly to himself to combat the negative thoughts.

"Have you realized that most of your unhappiness in life is due to the fact that you are listening to yourself instead of talking to yourself?" the author D. Martyn Lloyd-Jones writes.

"Take those thoughts that come to you the moment you wake up in the morning. You have not originated them, but they are talking to you, they bring back the problems of yesterday, etc. Somebody is talking. Who is talking to you? Your self is talking to you."[5] Lloyd-Jones points out that the writer of this psalm treats the ailment by talking back, by essentially saying to the fear, "Listen, you've talked long enough, but I am changing the story now. I am talking back, and I am switching the script."

At any moment, we can choose to start switching the script. The inner critic wants us to stay put and stagnant, but there is too much on the line to get complacent with these anthems of fear we've accepted for too long. What we're signing up for isn't a quick fix. Sadly, we cannot order a new mind-set from the drive-through with a side of fries. But day by day, we can make new choices and take new steps.

The story doesn't end when the heads are anointed with oil. There's a semicolon there. The sentence isn't over. The psalmist goes on to write, "My cup overflows." The promise for you and me is *overflow*. I know that feels hard to believe sometimes, but what if we just decided to say to ourselves, "I am choosing to believe in the overflow instead of the scarcity of my fear. I am choosing better thoughts—moment by moment—and I give myself loads of grace for the days I don't get it right. I am choosing to switch the script when the fear tries to hold me back because there are better anthems for me, and I am going to sing those anthems out loud."

We were made to sing better anthems, and every anthem starts with a single note.

Part 2

GO

Start
slow. Start
small. Dig deep. Sit
down. Say yes. Lock
eyes with God. It's
already in you.

Chapter 4

Commit to Mile One

For as long as I can remember, my favorite hobby has been transformation. Yes, as in the literal act of changing and becoming a better version of yourself.

I love to change. I love betterment and evolving. Becoming something new. I became a self-help junkie at the age of ten, and the idea that one could change and become a different and better version of themselves was absolutely addicting to me.

I was that kid who could not wait for summer vacation, but it wasn't because I wanted to have pool parties or get a break from schoolwork. Summer vacation was a luscious span of three months where I could become whoever I wanted to be. It was enough time—a golden chunk of ninety days—to undergo a serious transformation. I envisioned my classmates turning their heads and whispering to one another, "Is that Hannah? Can you believe it? She looks so cool this year."

Admittedly, nothing really changed. But there was always the allure that maybe this would be the year I'd come back to school with whiter teeth, a better haircut, a cooler wardrobe, or more confidence.

I was so committed the summer going into fourth grade and somehow got this idea in my head that I could become one of the popular girls by wearing neon clothing. I thought this was the thing. My childhood neighbors still like to remind me that

I announced to them while waiting at the bus stop on the first day of school, "So I am probably not going to have much time to spend with you guys anymore. This year is the year I become popular."

You could say transformation is in my DNA. I still haven't grown out of this feeling that if you would just give me ninety days or a six-week program, I could be a different person. I won't flinch at purchasing something new if it delivers a promise to me. I'm who the people have in mind when they write their marketing copy because I am bought into the idea of becoming someone new. I'm so bought in.

But here's what I'm learning in all of that: You can buy every program in the world and it still might not change anything. You can try the latest diet or buy the latest course. But unless you resolve to change something from the inside out, to make the journey deeper than skin-deep, you may always be looking for that next thing that promises to make you okay with yourself at long last.

All that to say, I've failed a million times to make literal change or progress in my health journey. When Lane and I first became engaged, I wanted to lose some weight for the wedding. It wasn't about fitting into a dress. I wanted to feel good instead of constantly feeling sluggish and tired. But I didn't make the right choices to get to that place.

I had a friend who, at the time, told me maybe the reason I wasn't losing weight was because of my medication. I'd been taking it for the last year to combat depression, and I kept thinking, *Maybe she's right. Maybe this is the thing holding me back from what I want.*

What followed was a series of stupid mistakes as I started weaning myself off my medication without the help of anyone around me. I didn't tell anyone. I just believed I could do it all on my own.

Things went downhill quickly. Within the span of a few weeks, I was feeling anxious again. I was struggling to stay focused. A thick fog of sadness settled over me. There was one day in particular when I started having a panic attack in my gym, thinking to myself, *I'm going back into the dark. Dear God, help me. I don't want to go back into the dark place.*

My therapist, who'd formed a relationship with me, phoned a doctor friend. The doctor, who normally had a wait list six months out, was able to get me in for a visit six weeks later. In the meantime, I went back on my medication. It was an act of faith for me. It was a step toward choosing to get better instead of wanting to look better.

I had to move some big boulders and get to the point of realizing that this wasn't about losing weight. It wasn't about a bikini. It wasn't about fixing something on the outside when all of it had to do with internal stuff I was facing. This had to do with my health—the most precious thing I could take care of. It had to do with my daily walk through depression and the shifts I could make to make the walk easier. This was bigger than a pants size.

"Working out will be medicinal for you," the new doctor told me as I sat in her office after that six-week wait. "People who go through depressive episodes are twice as likely to come out of them when they work out five days a week for forty-five minutes as compared to four days a week for thirty minutes."

It was there in my new doctor's office, watching her fill out another prescription for me, that I realized there were no quick fixes. It was going to be a slow, steady journey to being my best self, and it had nothing to do with a wedding dress.

Enter my too kind fiancé, who immediately stepped in to help me get back on track with working out just a month before the wedding. Deciding to push one another through workouts when you're in the midst of an engagement season is not something I would recommend to anyone, but we needed this. And trust me, it's a marvel that he was waiting there for me on our wedding day because during our workouts I would morph into the most awful person.

I still remember that first workout together. I spit. I cried. Every exercise felt more painful than the next. I was pushing against myself and could feel a tangible resistance bundled up inside of me. Lane kept pushing and cheering me on.

"Remember that time you showed up for Brooke at mile 19?" he said to me.

He was referring to something that had recently happened. My friend Brooke was training for a marathon, and during her twenty-mile training run, I promised to meet her at the park where she was running and run the last mile with her. Mile 19. That day was an absolute mess of tears and struggle for Brooke, but I made sure she crossed the finish line. I made sure she accomplished what she had come to do when all her inner voices were begging her to quit.

"Yes, I remember that!" I screamed back at him. "I remember mile 19, and it has nothing to do with this." At this point, I didn't want an inspirational story to get me through the workout.

"Well, push harder," Lane said to me as we transitioned into mountain climbers on the yoga mat. "This isn't your mile 19; this is your mile 1."

And oh, did the floodgates open up at this point! The tears came rushing out at the sound of those words: This isn't your mile 19; this is your mile 1.

I didn't want to be at mile 1. No one wants to be at mile 1. Mile 1 feels like an eternity; it feels like you are never going to finish. Nothing about the beginning of a journey feels sexy. There's nothing to boast over. There's no testimony post for mile 1.

I often don't even tell people about mile 1—that I even bothered to start—because I am usually fearful that I will quit the next day. I've made so many promises to myself that I haven't kept, and I can only imagine how damaging it is for my psyche, how much therapy I need for that treasure trove of unkept promises.

"Mile 1," he keeps saying as we lift and row and lunge our way to the end of that workout. "Mile 1. You're at mile 1."

Mile 1. This may be where you are right now, at the very beginning of everything that is about to unfold.

Mile 1 is wobbly.

Mile 1 is sort of embarrassing.

Mile 1 is the point in the story where all the voices will conspire in your brain to try to tell you, "Don't even bother. You can't do this. Change is just too hard." But there's the only person who can reach the mile marker—it's *you*. You're responsible for strapping on that mile tracker and beginning to run toward something new.

I know how hard this can be in a world that loves to celebrate people who cross the finish line, but here's something to remember as you move toward your goals: Every foot moved forward stacks up. It's all progress. And maybe you can't see the results just yet, but things are happening on the inside of you. Every time you show up to the task, you are becoming a different person who does not quit at the first sign of difficulty.

These tiny decisions made hourly and daily will one day be

the culmination of who you are five or ten years down the road. It all begins with declaring deep within yourself, *I'm in. I am going to run my race and run it well.*

In 1 Corinthians 9:24–27, the apostle Paul gets very clear about running our own races. He uses a lot of "Nike" verbiage when he's writing this section. But he gets very clear about how we run in the race to win the prize. And that's all you get control over—how you show up to run your race.

You don't control how other people train. You don't control whether you win or lose. You don't control where you place in the race. All you can control is what you do every single morning, afternoon, and evening to train for your race. All you control is how you invest in your own becoming. These words make me ask deeper questions:

> *What distracts me and gets in the way of my setting out to do this?*
> *What is working right now?*
> *What is definitely not working?*
> *Who can I be accountable to?*
> *How can I measure the progress?*
> *What am I willing to sacrifice for this?*
> *How far am I willing to go?*

These were just the basic questions, but they made me stare at myself and change some things. Because I want to be a doer. I've heard it said that the only thing that separates the doers from the dreamers is that doers actually do things. They set out. They start. They commit.

All day long, you can choose to present yourself to the world in whatever way you want to. You can edit the story. You can edit the photos. You can change the details or exaggerate in one area or another. But there's something entirely different about committing yourself to a daily grind. To renouncing the smoke and mirrors you apply to your own life and just deciding to lace up your shoes and start at mile 1.

That first mile likely won't be sexy or beautiful. You may have to stop and then start again, then stop and start once more. You may even keep it to yourself and not tell a soul you're at mile 1. That's okay. Lock eyes with God. He knows where you're at, and he knows that the beginning doesn't need to be beautiful.

There are no guidelines or rules for how it needs to look. Don't let the world fool you into thinking progress must look a certain way. Just be willing to dig deep and say to yourself, *This is my race. I'm not making excuses anymore. Here's my mile 1.*

And one last traveler note before you set out to do these things: Your worthiness and how you see yourself are two very different things. I say that because for a long time, I got that wrong. I assumed the view of myself, as unhealthy as it was, determined my worth. I thought the two were interchangeable.

Right now, you may see yourself as weak or disappointment. You may have a really hard time saying any sort of kind collection of words to yourself. But this talk—this negative view of yourself—has nothing to do with your worthiness.

Your worth does not come from how you make the journey look or whether you fall or trip along the way. Your worth does not come from what's on the other side of the mirror. Your worth could never be embedded in such trivial things. Your worthiness is with you regardless, hanging around your neck like a medal you already won. Your worth isn't fickle, but it may be something you need to learn to rehearse to yourself.

No matter what you do, not a person or a thing or an event

can take that worthiness away from you. But there is a way to make that sense of belief in yourself stronger and more durable. Your belief in yourself will only become more resilient as you dedicate yourself. It will expand as you get out there and start to track the miles. Even if you have to walk or limp your way past that first mile marker, it counts. It all counts, and no one can take that away from you.

Chapter 5

Take the Vitamins

The best stuff is always difficult. It takes longer. It requires practice and slow cooking. But slow simmering isn't a bad thing—that's where all the good things are blending together to make a finished product. Most of the time, to get to a place of rich results, you have to show up daily to the transformation.

When Lane and I first got married, I discovered a vitamin company that promised to make taking daily vitamins easier. I read that as, "We will do the hard work for you."

They got me. Hook, line, and sinker—they outlined all the reasons I have tried and failed at taking vitamins. Too many bottles. Too many brands. Too many pills. Too much money. This vitamin company promised to do all the hard work for me.

It started with a quiz online, and there's nothing I love more than a good quiz. The quiz spit back several vitamins I needed to be taking to reach my health goals. The bonus was that the box the vitamins came in was beautiful and every pack of vitamins came in individual packages with my name on it. For someone who likes packaging, this was a booby trap I would not be able to get around. I needed these vitamins in my life.

My friends and I joke that I am a multilevel marketer's dream because I buy in at the very start. You hardly have to sell me for even five minutes before I'm buying your face creams, your fitness programs, your oils. I buy in to anything that promises a future me.

So the vitamins for future me within the beautiful box showed up a few days later.

And I started taking them. And I think I fiddled more with the box and where to place it on the counter than I cared about the vitamins inside the box.

I imagine what happened next is that I missed a day of vitamins. And then another. And then, eventually the same thing happened that always happened with the vitamins: I forgot about them entirely. I didn't set reminders in my phone. I carried these little vitamin packs around with me and on trips, but I took them only occasionally when I would remember.

The beautiful boxes kept coming (because that's the model of a subscription service), and Lane patiently stacked box after box in our pantry. Once in a while, he'd nudge me and ask, "Have you taken your vitamins lately?"

Sidenote: I am well aware that I should have canceled this subscription, but I kept telling myself, *This will be the month when you take the vitamins, so keep on ordering them.*

Every time I opened the pantry, I'd be confronted with the beautiful boxes. I moved those boxes to a place I didn't access nearly as often as the pantry to avoid the taunting I could hear from the vitamin D and the fish oil, the two of them laughing at the fact that I would never change.

When we packed up our loft to move, I was forced to face the six-month supply of vitamins in the pantry.

Now here's the part of the story I hate telling, but I am an honest storyteller: I was an evangelist for these vitamins. I was a hard-core cheerleader. I talked them up to people. I was so enamored by the benefits I wasn't even experiencing that I wanted all the people around me to have them. And they did. My friends gobbled it up, and they too started getting boxes delivered to their doorsteps. But the difference was that they took the vitamins. They did the most important part. They experienced the full benefits.

The vitamin company could deliver some solid packaging. They could divide the vitamins into little packets. They could even put my name on said packets. Really, they could not have made the process any easier for me. But at the end of the day, none of it would have mattered if I failed to open the packet and swallow the vitamins.

The easiest solutions can be delivered to our doorsteps, but consistency—and everything it takes to be a disciplined person—still isn't something we can order off Amazon. That requires work. That requires showing up.

This is hard for someone who is a recovering "I want to see results immediately" addict. I feel like I have the credibility to say this because I spent a summer working at the headquarters of "'Oh, You Will See Results Immediately': As Seen on TV." For an entire summer, I peddled broken solutions to people who wanted one-minute abs, Michelle Obama arms, and ripe overnight tomatoes—all without doing any work. I did not want to hear from anyone that I would have to "keep at it" and "keep going back" to ever see the results I wanted for my life.

Take the dumb vitamins, for instance—it takes time for the vitamins to do their job. You cannot just take them once or twice or every three weeks and expect the results they promise. You need to take them daily, as consistently as you can, until you start to see the changes from the inside out.

Research shows it can take anywhere from two to six weeks to start to experience the benefits of supplements. In some cases, you need to take the supplements regularly for ninety days before you start to feel the difference. When you're someone who loves instant results, this can be disheartening to hear. But what if, one step at a time, you started steadily stepping out on the path toward consistency? What if you decided that, no matter how hard it was, you were going to keep moving forward anyway?

I've been forced to learn this lesson of "keeping at it" in multiple areas of my life, especially any instance that involves me and a kitchen. My husband is a master chef, and on our third date he cooked me a decadent, candlelit meal of scallops and orzo pasta and then asked me to bring the dessert. I, like the peasant I am in the kitchen, showed up with a brownie mix in a box.

This continued for all of our dating history. He would show off in the kitchen, and I would flounder because I hated following directions and all the steps that came with the recipes. One time, I decided I was going to break this curse that existed between me and the kitchen. I planned a lengthy menu and gave myself two hours (that was the first mistake). We were going to dine on burgers filled with gouda, scalloped sweet potatoes, and roasted broccoli. I pushed the couch out of the way, set a blanket on the floor, lit some candles, and prepared for our indoor picnic.

The menu sounds delicious, I know, but I can promise you that it was one of the most atrocious meals we've ever had. The potatoes were hard. The burgers were dry. The broccoli was bland.

"It seems like you had some pretty good recipes," Lane said to me. "I wonder why things went so wrong."

"It's because I'm tired," I snapped back at him. "And I was too tired to keep following all the steps in the recipe so I just started to improvise. I just wanted the food to be done."

We live in a world where the noodles come prepared and the veggies come prechopped. And that's not to say it's a bad thing, but the drive-through culture and instant access mentality make it hard to think about slowing down to go step-by-step.

If you're like me, you may feel pressure from a society that looks like everyone is a finished product and you're just the half-assembled desk from IKEA. You may see people at the "top level" and shame yourself for not being where they are. But let me tell you the truth: to get to the top of the ladder, you start at the bottom rung.

The daily vitamin. The printing of the recipe. The first workout. Genesis 1.

And then you take those small things and put them on repeat. Discipline stacks up, and those results will come with enough time and enough daily application. Eventually, your feelings of being overwhelmed will start to fade and you'll miss fewer days and all the small things will morph into habits. And those habits will set you up for rhythms. And those rhythms become anthems you know by heart. And those anthems have the potential to power you into such greatness you cannot even fathom right now.

What you will see up ahead as you acquire a taste for small things on repeat is that virtually everything is just a bunch of small stuff that looks big when you put it all together. And then when you read the Bible, you will notice that God is a God of small things, just as much as he is the God of big miracles. And the beautiful realization comes when you start to see that this idea of "small things on repeat" extends so much further than daily disciplines like meditation or going for a run. You will begin to notice that everything hinges on coming back tomorrow to keep the results coming. You will start to see prayer as something you visit daily. Forgiveness is something you take as a daily supplement. Hope is something you have to rehearse daily. Community is held together by regular check-ins and gatherings. All the beautiful things of this life that God intends for us to live into come with a bunch of "rinse and repeat for best results" instructions.

So start small. And don't belittle that first vitamin or that first page you read after spending four years only reading textbooks for school. Read the page, and then give yourself a high five or a fist bump because this is your progress. This is your race.

And no matter what anyone tries to tell you, you are not racing against the world. You are competing against only one thing: who you were yesterday. Today is a chance to start being a little better, a little more disciplined, or a little kinder.

And here's the thing. We are constantly hearing the message, "You don't need to change because you are good as you are." That's not a bad message, but I don't want to stay just as I am. I want to evolve. I want to keep getting better. I want to uncover new levels.

I want to grow kinder and softer. I want to unlock new parts of my heart. I want to encounter new levels of prayer and intimacy with God. I want to fill more notebooks and write more words. I want to burn more eggs and attempt, once again, to make grain-free pancakes. I want to take pictures and love people and host parties and say sappy things to my husband. I want to light candles at dinner and make amends when it's necessary. I want to feel every angle of humanity and really be a part of it while I'm here.

I want to know what my best life could feel like, and I want to step into every gorgeous thing that is waiting for me up ahead. I know there is more up ahead. And so I'm taking my vitamins and getting back to work.

Chapter 6

Lay the Bricks

Last year, Lane and I began the process of preparing to buy a house. What no one ever told me was what a draining and emotionally exhausting thing this whole process is. Lane insisted I be a part of it, and I kept asking him if he could just buy the house without telling me and then surprise me, like in one of those home makeover shows.

As I scrolled through Zillow, I discovered a house that seemed perfect. Almost too perfect. It had been on the market for the last three months, and of course, I took that as a sign that it was waiting for us. I did the one thing you are never supposed to do when you set out into the jungle of home buying: I fell in love with a house that didn't belong to us.

It was one of the houses where you can text a number and get a door code to enter at any time. So I did that. A bunch. I would walk the space. I would sit in the "living room." I would spend time on the back deck. I'm sure multiple neighbors saw me and thought, *Again? That girl is back again?*

I saw myself prepping dinner at the kitchen counter. I saw kids in a nursery. I married that home in my mind. Every time I checked, the home was still on the market, and I thought to myself, *This is it. This home is waiting for us.*

That next week, Lane's best friend Nick came to stay with us for a weekend. We took him to see the house. My dream home.

My forever home. I stood in the doorway waiting for him to grab my shoulders and scream at me, "THIS IS IT. GO, CHILD. GO!" But he did nothing of the sort.

Instead, he and Lane began to walk around the house. Soon enough, their whole demeanor had changed. They started pointing out little flaws. Shoddy craftsmanship. Uneven beams. The light switches were even crooked.

Nick didn't grab my shoulders. He simply looked at us and said, "It's not a good investment. This isn't the home you want to move into."

I was crushed. Instead of listening to him, I secured my justification hat firmly on my head and started going back at him. "But that's so small . . . we could fix that . . . we could handle that."

Nick interrupted me. "If the little things need this much care and attention, you can only imagine what a nightmare the house is at its foundation."

That house didn't end up becoming our home. The truth is, the home sat on the market for even longer. It went off the market and then back on again a few weeks later. It turns out the home did not sell until the sellers were willing to do some serious foundational work.

The foundation building is never the fun part of the story because it's not what people see. It's not a finished product; it's the seemingly boring start to one.

The foundation will determine how the rest of the house holds itself up. The foundation determines longevity. And sometimes the builder has no choice but to demolish the whole thing because the foundation is just not sturdy enough to carry what is on the way.

Right before I uprooted my life in Connecticut and moved

to Atlanta, I attended a conference in North Carolina with one of my best friends. I was about to move across the country, and she was moving back to her home state of Maine, so we decided to take a trip together in case we didn't get to see one another as often as we had.

We ordered a red convertible as a rental car at the airport and made our way around Raleigh. We took our time that week leading up to the conference, slowly sipping our coffees, staying up late to hash out dreams for the future, forgetting to check our phones.

We sat at dinner with two heaping bowls of clams and pasta between us. I decided to say something out loud—something I was afraid of saying but didn't want to keep to myself anymore.

"I'm so afraid I'm going to miss life," I told her. "I'm afraid to find out that maybe I'm chasing all the wrong things and they'll never make me happy. I will never reach that point of contentment."

She nodded across the table from me. The nod told me everything I needed to know—she felt it too. She was stuck in the same cycle of chasing things and coming up empty.

I was unbalanced, but no one could see it. On the outside, I looked like I had it all together. But behind the scenes, I was filled with fear of failing. I was barely sleeping. I was living each day with bad habits, crawling to the finish line of each midnight hour and wondering why this wasn't filling me anymore. Turns out, I wasn't afraid of missing my life. I was already missing it by being too invested in what everyone else was doing and how I could have the same kind of success they were having. The foundation for my life was anything but sturdy.

At the end of the first day of the conference, the presenters asked us to spread out across the hotel ballroom where we'd been dreaming and plotting all day. They instructed us to lie down in an open space, close our eyes, and let the noise of the "to do" and the "must do" fall away.

I remember thinking this was a ridiculous task I wasn't up for. I was tempted to go to the bathroom during this time because I don't like to daydream. More than that, I don't like sitting still. I want to be up and doing something. I was exhausted at this point, and the silence plus the chance to think hit me harder than I was expecting. I could feel the tears welling up in my eyes the moment I placed my head on the floor.

They invited us to imagine our lives, to get a clear picture in our heads of what we wanted them to look like five years from now.

The picture that came into my brain must have been hand-packaged and plopped into an Amazon Prime box by God because I would never have thought of it on my own. I saw a house with a big countertop. I saw him. A man. The two of us. We were sitting side by side on the countertop, legs swinging. I saw no urgency at the moment. No phones present. Nowhere to be but right here. My head was on his shoulder. The only light in the room came from white Christmas lights we had never bothered to take off the windows after the holiday ended.

We were sitting there together, and I thought it was just the two of us, but then people started coming in. I didn't know who the people were, but I assumed they were friends—people we'd met along the way. Everyone was so happy. Everyone was laughing and genuinely enjoying each other's company. There was nowhere to be. We were surrounded. It felt like warmth and peace and everything I didn't know I wanted.

Before long, I was weeping on the floor of the hotel ballroom. Audibly crying. I mean, I'm sure people were staring. My chest was heaving. The tears were hot. As crazy as it sounds, that was the moment I realized I needed to change my entire life.

I was finally awake to the truth I'd been pushing down: My life looks nothing like how I want it to look five years from now. Nothing in my life currently looks as if I would ever want to settle down, have a family, or be surrounded by people who love me. I don't even know how to get to that place.

Five years since lying on that hotel ballroom floor, I am in that house. I have that countertop that wraps around the kitchen. I am with that man. The lights are here. The people surround us, and we feel at home and safe among them. But here's the thing. It's not about the house or the countertop. It has nothing to do with physical things. What I saw on that hotel floor was a vision of a life that was better for me, healthier. I saw a vision of life where I felt rooted and home, surrounded and plugged into a bigger sense of community. But no, it wasn't the picture I'd planned for myself all along. It wasn't anything I would have told you I wanted while I was busy hustling to get the next big thing done.

I say this because the vision didn't easily assemble itself. It was unbearably hard, and it meant the entire foundation I'd built for myself that relied on busyness, efficiency, metrics, and accolades needed to be smashed to the ground and a new foundation needed to be built, brick by brick.

This work was painful. It was hard. It required lots of therapy and honest conversations. There was no perfect path, and there still isn't. But when I think I'm running out of direction or maybe going in the wrong one, God hands me another brick. I realize I am building with bricks now. They are weighty and permanent. They are lasting and not easily shaken. They require more precision and more time. But because of those bricks and the time it took to lay them, I've become unshakable.

I want you to know it's never too late. You are never too far gone to start laying the brick or start from scratch. After God promised Jeremiah he would rebuild the city's ruins, Nehemiah stepped in to oversee the work. I am sure at that point there were plenty of people thinking or even saying out loud, "Really? You are going to invest your time in building a wall that was already knocked down?"

At one point in Nehemiah's building process, his enemies showed up to taunt him and try to get him to come down from his work in progress. Nehemiah yelled down to all the naysayers, "I'm doing a great work; I can't come down." Bit by bit, he kept laying the brick until the work was finished. In just fifty-two days, Nehemiah rebuilt the city wall.

People won't always understand your new commitments or growing devotion. They might make comments. They might not ask about it at all. But you don't have to play small to please people who don't "get it." You don't have to be sorry for saying, "I am doing something great, and I can't stop doing it right now."

Keep on laying the brick and allowing God to establish that work in you.

It's okay if the work seems impossible.

It's okay if the vision changes.

It's okay if you found yourself fighting for what you thought was important only to have the direction change.

It's okay if you decide you want to fight for something different. Something slower. Something messier. Something more real.

It is never too late to change directions. It is never too late to forge a new path.

That word *forge*—it's a special one for me. To forge a new path is to toil and work to create something new, somewhere that never existed before. But the word *forge* originally came from the blacksmith—how the blacksmith would heat and hammer and form iron into different shapes to fit a new purpose. That was the original meaning of the word *forge*.

And that may be what you feel as you go through the heat and the hard stuff to get to the other side. You may feel like you're being battered into shape or experiencing some kind of fire. The heat, though it hurts, is beautiful and necessary. Don't shy away from what the blacksmith wants to do, how he wants to shape you and prep you and ultimately fit you for a new purpose. Don't be scared off from going back to the foundation and painstakingly laying down new bricks. Each brick will hold meaning. Each brick will hold weight. And layer by layer, you'll become unshakable.

Chapter 7

Say Yes to Slow Magic

Just before Lane started a new job this past year, he decided to take one of his last days off to go golfing. His golf clubs sit in the back of the garage collecting dust, but on rare occasions, he pulls them out and hits the course.

This is what I love about Lane—he never lets inexperience keep him from showing up to any occasion. I've sat on the idea of taking a dance class in Atlanta for the last three years, but it's always the fear that I'm going to be rusty or not make any friends that keeps me from ever pulling the tap shoes out of the closet and showing up.

Lane doesn't care. He doesn't care if it isn't his best round of golf, and he is fine to go off and play solo. So that's what he did. Hours later, Lane came home and told me he'd made two friends named Betsy and Joe. They invited him to play golf with them and then extended the invitation further by asking him to officially become a part of a cornhole league for the summer with them. This is my husband. He makes friends with walls and somehow leaves the house for three hours and comes back on an official cornhole team.

When I met Betsy for the first time a few weeks later at one of those cornhole matches, I understood how Lane was so easily adopted on the golf range by two people who saw him swinging alone.

"Come on," they called to him. "You're playing with us today."

Betsy is a presence. She will immediately shake your hand and draw you into her circle. Instantly, you are one of Betsy's clan members. By the end of the night, we were sitting on the steps of the restaurant after the cornhole matches, eating fried cauliflower and playing matchmaker for another member of the cornhole team.

"So Lane tells me he's in a softball league come fall, and it's on Thursday nights, just like cornhole," Betsy mentioned to me on the steps. "So I guess that means you're joining the team in his place?"

I don't know if my face locked up at that moment, but I'm sure I started making all sorts of motions with my hands. Like, *No, I am not joining your team.* All these memories of kickball games gone awry in the third grade came flooding back to me.

"You don't want me on your team," I told Betsy. "I'm not good."

This was one of those moments I needed to remember so I could haul it to my therapist's office the following week. It's a pattern I don't just see in myself but in a lot of other people I meet. The uncertainty. The willingness to put yourself down without flinching. The lie taking over the story line that you are "not good" and there is no debate for whether you can improve or not. In reality, I think a cornhole league could be fun, but I have spent years not moving into things that interest me because I'm afraid I will not be "good" at them.

Betsy didn't care for any of my excuses.

"Come on," she said to me. "Let's go throw some bags before they pack up the boards."

She led me down to the spot where they had just played a

match an hour before, and she stood beside me at the front of the course.

"You played any sports growing up?"

"Just dance," I tell her.

"A ballerina?"

"A ballerina," I confirmed.

"Even better. You'll be great at this."

Betsy, who must have spent some of her days at the dance barre too, immediately coaxed me into fifth position and, having placed two beanbags in my hands, moved my arms into position in front of me. She demonstrated how I would glide from fifth position to fourth while moving my arm in a circular motion to launch the beanbag into the air.

"Your eyes are on the target," she said to me. "But it isn't about that right now; it's only about following through with the throw."

And with those instructions and the pressure taken off me, Betsy and I began launching beanbags into the air. We must have looked crazy standing in our ballet positions before winding up to throw. I didn't care though. I was enjoying the moment, and the feeling of needing to be good at something fell off of me.

I want to say I only hit the board twice after dozens of throws, but every time I threw the bag in the air and "followed through," Betsy would hoot and holler and high-five me. It had nothing to do with hitting the target; it was about the slow magic of mastering the very first step.

I'm sure you've heard it—the wildly popular and equally enticing myth that excellence happens overnight. That you can become who you were made to be and create the best stuff of your life instantly—without any practice. This is false advertising. I guarantee that anyone you see or admire, doing the very thing you desire to do, started with a wobbly first step and then spent hours and hours investing before the world ever noticed them.

We have to be people who love the practice above the finished product because the practice is where you meet God. It's where you become fully yourself. It's where you figure out what's on the inside and what you bring to the table.

Because you bring something valuable and necessary to the table, and it's not supposed to look like everyone else's dish.

Let's say I invite you to a dinner party at my home. I send you the link and ask you to sign up for something. I want to make sure the dishes on the table are diverse that night. You take a glance at the list and realize someone is bringing a unique appetizer. Bacon-wrapped dates (only because that's my favorite thing in the world). You wouldn't think to steal what they're making. You wouldn't double up on the bacon-wrapped dates, right? So why would you be willing to do the same thing with your calling? Why would you look to others to inform what you bring to the table?

If you spend your days focusing on what other people are doing, you'll miss what God wants to do with you. You'll miss the marrow. You'll miss what's unique about your story. And let's be honest, there is far too much imitation in the world already. What we need is people who are willing to get alone with God, dig deep, and figure out what they bring to the table. Because it's different from what someone else brings. The only way to figure out what that thing is? Invest in the secret hours.

With more than ten years of investing in my craft, I can tell you the magic lives in the secret hours. In the time invested in a process rather than a finished product. The magic will find you there. And if you let it, it will transform you on deep levels. It will make you feel more yourself than you can ever imagine.

If you are struggling to figure out what it is you want to invest in, I might nudge you with this: pick one thing. Just one thing. Maybe it's a workout program or a Bible study. Maybe you want to become a runner or you want to write that first page of the novel you've thought of writing for so many years. Pick one thing, and follow it long enough to see some discipline and results grow from the continual showing up to do the work that no one sees.

A woman once came up to me at a conference with a frantic look on her face as she told me, "I don't know what I am! I don't know who I should be! Am I a photographer? Am I a writer? Am I a podcast host? How did you know you were a writer?"

I could see the fear in her eyes, the fear that if she went down one path, then maybe she would miss all the others. I don't think God works that way, but I do think we need to invest long enough in one thing to figure out what it makes us feel.

"When I'm writing, I feel closer to God than when I'm doing any other thing," I told the woman. "And how could I not want to feel that feeling as much as possible?"

That was my simple answer, but it wasn't an overnight answer. It solidified itself over a decade of notes scribbled on napkins, bad stories, nights being unable to sleep over plotlines, and the continual showing up to plant my butt in the chair without any more excuses to hold me back. Every one of us has access to this.

You have permission to begin right where you are. In this very moment. And you can tell yourself, even if you don't believe it at first, "I am showing up for progress, not perfection. I am showing up, regardless of the pieces I cannot see in the puzzle yet. I believe in the magic that will come from the slow and steady path forward. This is between me and you, God. Let's do this thing."

Take that mentality with you and pack it in your gym bag.

Take that mentality with you and pour it into your morning coffee.

Take that mentality with you and give yourself grace when you try and then fumble on that first attempt.

Make it about you and God. Lock eyes. You're the only two people in the ring today.

It's not about the five hundred Facebook friends.

It's not about whoever does or does not watch your stories.

It isn't anyone watching—it's about doing it, even if no one ever comes to watch. You have to see the finish line for yourself and know you were born to cross it and experience the feeling of victory in your bones.

Becoming a better version of yourself is something you get to see the fruit of first. Just you. You'll be the first to experience that surge of magic. You're the one who plants the discipline; you're the one who sees the first sprout coming up from the ground. Not your boss. Not your mother. Not your husband. Not the Instagram world.

You get the first look of your own improvement—you and God. Let it be sacred, and celebrate the small victory. You planted something. You showed up. You dug in the dirt. You decided to keep showing up, despite the fear.

Transformation is a glorious thing, and we all have access to it. But you "get to" improve. You don't "have to" improve. You get to show up today. You get to invest in yourself today. You get to look different at the end of the day because of a series of small steps you chose and are continuing to choose.

Start slow. Start small. Dig deep. Sit down. Say yes. Lock eyes. Go.

It's already in you.

Chapter 8

Put Your Blinders On

People are going to try to take the wins away from you. It's just what people do when they aren't happy with themselves. They try to suck, suck, suck the joy from somebody else. They say when life gives you lemons, you make lemonade. Some people won't. Some people utterly despise lemonade. They spend the best hours of their day hurling rotten lemons at all the people out there running the race, and I can only imagine what a miserable hobby that is. To be on the sidelines with a bunch of rotten lemons and no real skin in the game.

These people are often living in the comments section on blogs or giving one-star reviews on Amazon. They're found angry-tweeting or cutting people off at red lights for no good reason. And it would be easy to expend all your energy on trying to figure out why they are the way they are, but that would only take away from why you're here today.

A couple of years ago, someone sent me an anonymous email with a link to a blog they'd created. Simply put, this blog was dedicated to telling the internet about how much I sucked (their words, not mine). Yes, this person dedicated hours of their life to creating a blog about why I was an awful human being. There were about a dozen posts, and a new one coming every time I pressed Publish on my blog. This person would attack my words, my content, and my character. They did this for a long time, and they kept sending emails to make sure I got the memo.

My "big sister" advice would be to tell you not to focus on the critics, but there is a chance you're going to have to feel the pain for yourself before you decide to turn the other cheek. It's like telling someone to stay away from the fire. We all need to figure out how the burn feels on our skin.

So, yes, I didn't listen to my own advice. I read the blogs as they published them. I absorbed them and allowed them to fill me with shame. I didn't think to open my mouth and tell anyone about the blog because I was afraid that maybe the words were true, maybe I *was* who this person thought I was. Maybe I *was* a fraud.

The bullying got worse. And though I don't know if the person who wrote the blog was the same person who sent me various anonymous emails, I have a hunch.

At one point in all of this, I finished writing my first book. I remember thinking, *Wow, I did this thing. And I want everyone else to know they can do it too.* I published a post about how, for the first time in my life, I finally felt truly brave. I felt unstoppable, and I wanted everyone to experience this same feeling of believing in themselves. In feeling the fear and doing it anyway.

And when I pressed Publish, the email from my anonymous internet friend showed up.

The core of the email was this: You are not brave. You might be this or you might be that, but you're not brave. And you shouldn't bother telling people you're brave because you're too young to be brave and life hasn't hit you fully enough for you to be brave and your life is too pretty to be brave. You need to do x, y, and z before you think you're brave.

I know these kinds of words from a stranger aren't supposed

to matter to me. I've read all the advice from other writers who suggest you just tack on the line, "Hi, I am a complete stranger dropping into your inbox to give you some advice on your own life," before you read a single sentence, and it will somehow soften the blow. But it doesn't take away from the truth: Words sting. Words cut. As one of my readers once told me, "Words can be weapons or balms, depending on how we use them." And it hurts to read what people think about you—whether they're addressing you out of truth, anger, jealousy, or genuine concern.

This wasn't the first mean email. And truth be told, it wasn't the worst email. I've gotten the threats and the people who show up in my inbox just to say, "I think you should die and make the world better." But this email was different. This one about the bravery bothered me and stuck with me. It made me angry. And I wasn't angry at the words they said; I was angry because I know the truth about bravery: You have no right to come alongside someone and tell them whether or not they've reached a level of bravery you approve of. You don't get to determine what does or does not make a person brave or lovely or worthy or good. That's not your right. That's not your calling. That's just a tactic to try to keep someone else from reaching their full potential. If you ask me, the world already has enough of that negativity floating around.

Here's the truth about bravery; here is her essence: She can't be defined by a measuring cup or a yardstick or a square foot. Bravery isn't the kind of thing you measure; it's the kind of thing you activate. It's pretty obvious to everyone that we walked into a life that isn't always kind or bearable or comfortable or good, and it takes a real chunk of bravery to just get through a day sometimes.

Bravery—if you ask me—is the day my best friend told me she was getting sober and I watched her hands tremble in anticipation of the hurdles of what would come next. Bravery—if you ask me—is watching a dear friend raise four beautiful children with all the grit she's got and showing up for those children even when she is tired and broken and worn. That, my friends, is Titanic-sized bravery to me.

Bravery—if you ask me—is the day he was diagnosed with cancer and the only response on his lips was this: "I will fight this thing. I will be relentless, and I will fight this thing." Bravery—if you ask me—is her showing up at my door, the one with the big red handle, and speaking the truth out loud: "I want more. I've been afraid to say it for a really long time, but I want more for this life of mine." Bravery is the places you went to when you were scared. Bravery is the day she called the therapist and finally made the appointment. Bravery isn't something anyone gets to define or measure; bravery is something you activate.

So, no, no one gets to tell you a hurdle that has taken you years to finally get over is something you should have learned to limbo under several yesterdays ago. That's not kind. That's not true. That's just playing small within a life that calls you to more.

And that is exactly the problem with the culture we're standing inside of today. We are constantly confronted by people who tell us that bravery is Elsewhere. And beauty is Elsewhere. And life, or a life you can be proud of, is Elsewhere. And Elsewhere is just a flimsy little measure we never plan to reach, but it does its justice in keeping us from showing up to the life we've been given for this moment. Elsewhere is just a defense mechanism that allows you to keep your fists clenched and your heart closed to what life could look like if you showed up and said yes to the beautiful now.

There are always going to be people who don't want you to show up. You cannot control their presence, but you can turn down the volume as they start to speak. For too long, I listened.

And it never made me happier. It actually got me to believe there was something inside me I needed to fix before I could offer anything to the world. It's wasted time trying to please people who can't be pleased, I learned. You won't suddenly arrive at a point of feeling worthy if your goal is to just fix all the stuff you think is wrong with you. There will always be another thing. There will always be another standard to distract you from the real work of this lifetime. Bet on that. But you have one road to focus on. One thing you came here for. Keep your eyes on that prize, and don't turn your head to the left or the right. Let them talk. Pay no attention to them. I know that's tricky, but it's vital if you want to keep moving forward.

I have a friend Felicia, who is my walking buddy. We meet up every month and take long walks around the neighborhood. She's older than me and has raised three children who are now off in the world making their own babies and being fantastic humans who care about others, and so I try to glean every ounce of wisdom I can get from Felicia.

One morning out on our walk, I opened up to Felicia about how I was having a hard time focusing because I kept taking my eyes off my tasks and placing them on other things.

"When my daughter was a little girl, she couldn't pay attention in math class for the life of her," Felicia starts telling me. "She could not keep her focus on the chalkboard because there were so many other distractions in the room. It was happening day after day. And so I had to start giving her a pep talk in the morning before she went off to school."

Felicia would bend down to her little girl's level and say to her, "Blinders on, baby. Blinders on."

Blinders originated with horses. These small leather patches are attached to a horse's head so they stay on course. The blinders are placed on them to keep them on track, to keep them from looking to the left and right of them.

Here's what I didn't know about blinders though. The old story goes that blinders were invented by a preacher who made a bet with a friend that he could get his horse to walk up the stairs in his home. The horse did this with no problems at all, but when the preacher tried to get the horse down the stairs, he wouldn't budge. The preacher covered the horse's head and led him down the stairs. It was there that he realized that by covering all or part of the horse's vision, he could get the horse to take chances he normally would not take.

This is what happens when we put the blinders on and keep them on. We start to take chances we normally wouldn't take. With the voices of fear and hate not being able to get past the blinders, we get a little bolder. We activate a little more bravery. We start to think that maybe, just maybe, it matters that we are here and some good, good work can finally be done.

When they're hurling rotten lemons at you, take those lemons and squeeze them for all the juice they've got inside them—waiting to be tapped into. Take another step. Write another article. Publish another anthem. Find another avenue. Just keep going—no matter the adversity.

This world is full of needs. Your existence and your creations fill some of those needs. Your showing up and doing your job fill those needs. Your kindness and your ability to make people feel seen fill those needs. Focus more on those needs than on the people who try to shut you down. There will always be critics and haters who will make their opinions known. You can't stop them anyway, so channel that energy back into why you're here. Shake it off, and put the blinders on.

Blinders on, baby. Blinders on.

Chapter 9

Promise Me You'll Fail

I want to reintroduce you to someone.

It's likely you've met him before at parties or school events. It's someone who, once you first heard about him from other people, you decided you wanted nothing to do with him.

Failure. That's his name.

You don't like the way he looks, and I don't blame you. You don't like how his name sounds coming off the tongue. Chances are, you've done everything possible to avoid this guy because you fear what we all fear: being associated with him.

This is why the reintroduction is necessary because this guy has been misunderstood. He has been demonized and ostracized when in reality he brings something valuable to the table. He is someone you want to listen to and learn from. He needs a turn to speak.

I don't know when it starts becoming hardwired in our brains to avoid Failure, but I know I spent half of my life trying to avoid him at all costs out of fear that someone might notice me with him. Maybe it's all the pressure to pass tests and fill our report cards with letters that are all very close to the beginning of the alphabet. Maybe it's the way we're measured against one another from a young age with comments that seem harmless until they grow up to shape an identity.

I don't know when Failure becomes the true enemy; I just

know I spent all of my teens and half of my twenties trying to avoid it at all cost. I know I wasn't very good at being rejected or getting harsh criticism. Those are the kinds of things that shut me down, and I just didn't know at the time that I could grow a thicker skin and get over it. I held on tight to every defect I encountered within myself. I kept myself on a tight regimen of overachieving and performing for approval. And then when I was twenty-six, everything crashed. I reached the "rock bottom" that people talk about, and it left me in a state where I couldn't sleep, couldn't process thoughts, couldn't work, and couldn't perform. Suddenly it was no longer about perfection—it was about survival. As a severe depression swept over me, I suddenly understood why some people just can't get up in the morning, how their brain is so tired and not another message to "get stronger" or "improve their life" is going to make any difference. All I wanted during that dark time was for someone to hold me and tell me, "It's okay if you can't fight your way out of these woods. I'll stay with you in the dark until you're ready to move."

When I went to the hospital for my severe depression, I ended up getting referred to an inpatient program where I would get my life back on the rails. I would participate in therapy. I would meet with the counselors. I would dedicate myself to healing and group talk and health. I want to be honest in saying that I was deeply ashamed. Even though shame deserved no place in my story, I couldn't help but think I'd let myself down. At that point in my life, sitting in the waiting room beside all these other people I never thought I'd have something in common with, I felt like I was a failure. Like, how did I end up here? Like, what had I done to end up in this place?

The shame was heavy on me, and I kept trying to figure my way out of it. I would have told you, if you had been sitting beside me in that waiting room as I filled out all sorts of papers and signed my life away to doctors I didn't know, that this was a failure. This was the thing I feared the most—not being able to control my own life and needing others to help me put it back together again.

My compassionate side, which doesn't come out all that often, would have told a different story—one in which I would be able to tell myself that this is a bump in the road. And I can't swerve away from it. And I can't dodge it. So we are going to move through it. There's no other way—we must move through it. My compassionate side wasn't present on that day.

Looking back, I realize that going where there was help wasn't a failure. The only person condemning me at that moment was myself. And I think if Failure would have been the one sitting beside me in the waiting room, watching people shuffle in and out with bags of medicine in hand, he would have tapped my shoulder and said, "You've got me all wrong, kid. I'm nothing to fear. I am just someone who shows up to teach you about yourself. Without me, you could very well stay the same person for a long time—and how boring would that become?"

It took me years and many attempts at sacrificing my perfectionist self to reframe failure and give it ample room to spread out. Turns out, I wasn't afraid to fail. It wasn't that at all. I had a collection of failures I would even say I was proud of. But what I was desperately afraid of, what needed to change, was how I viewed myself in light of the failure. How I defined myself based on failure. How I was quick to be compassionate with other people in my life who failed big and failed hard, but I was brutal when I was the one who hit the bump in the road.

Something beautiful happened when I was forced to face myself with humility and grace for the road I was on. When

I had to tap in deep and figure out where my compassion for myself existed. And I'll be honest with you—I didn't have much compassion stocked up for myself. Something within me had to die before I could truly apply compassion to myself.

This need to be everything to everyone had to die. The need to impress everyone around me, the need to perform for love, had to be sacrificed to officially move past this. Because here I was, in a state where I could not offer anyone anything, and I was learning, through every humble movement, that people still showed up to love me. It wasn't the droves of people who follow along on social media. It was the people who still wanted me, even if I could never do a single thing to return their love. My thinking I needed to perform for love and worthiness was simply a fear-filled anthem I had constructed for myself. It was a horrible song, and I danced to the tune for far too long, though I never really liked the way it sounded as it came through the speakers.

I've learned so much since that day in the waiting room:

- I've learned you can't wish the best for others but believe you deserve nothing at all.
- I've learned you can't truly love people at full capacity if you hate yourself.
- I've learned you can't say failure is necessary for other people but reject yourself when it comes to court you.
- I've learned you can't hate your way into love, growth, or progress. It doesn't work that way. You must partner with yourself, even at the rock-bottom moments, and allow God to pull you up to new levels.

The news is official: you're going to fail.

You will encounter Failure in all sorts of ways. You'll forget someone's birthday. You'll forget someone's name. You'll get lost. You'll be late because you got lost. Sometimes you won't show up at all.

You'll make a mistake. You'll hurt someone who means the world to you. It'll feel like a brick sitting in the inside of your stomach. You'll never want to hurt another person again. But you will. And you'll be hurt. You will be rejected or not picked for the team. Someone will talk about you behind your back. You will make the same mistake and talk about someone else.

You'll fail a test. You'll stay up studying all night and draw a blank in the morning. You'll oversleep. You'll break a promise. You'll break a heart. You'll let go—even when both of you want to hold on longer.

You'll miss out. You'll miss an opportunity. You will be slow to forgive. You'll regret someone. You may be the regret of someone else.

You will be criticized. You will be pushed against. You won't be the life of the party. Sometimes you won't even get the invite.

You're going to fail. And as long as you don't take those failures and stack them on your chest like badges of shame that discount you from this life, you will be okay. You will grow from this. Your failures are not badges of shame. It's better than that. Those bright and colorful patches on your chest are badges of honor.

As I add another badge to myself, I try to breathe deep and say with all the compassion I can muster, "That happened." Swallow hard. Suck in more air. Nod your head. "Yes, that happened. And this thing can only take me out of the running for my own life if I choose to let it shut me down." I can either view this failure as the end of me, or I can look at it from every angle and ask myself a better question: "What did we learn?"

That's where the compassion doubles in size when I choose to partner with myself instead of point fingers at the shortcomings.

What are we still learning?

What will we be learning for a very long time because this happened?

It's in these moments that I realize I want and need Failure in my story because I learn the most when I fall and then get back up and keep going.

Seth Godin said, "The rule is simple: The person who fails the most will win. If I fail more than you do, I will win. Because in order to keep failing, you've got to be good enough to keep playing."[6]

Maybe that's the message we need to know: we are good enough to keep playing.

We are good enough to keep going.

We are good enough to strip off the perfectionist mentality and pick up the glove.

We are good enough so strap on our cleats and our kneepads and get back on the field.

Several years ago, a young woman interned with me for the summer. She was my first intern as a self-employed person, but I had plenty of experience leading interns during my first job out of college. One of the things I remember most from that time was all the paperwork the interns were required to sign before they could officially begin. And none of that paperwork made them any less nervous. When they first came to me, they looked like, well, how I looked at my first internship. Nervous. Afraid. Terrified to make a wrong move. And I never did know how to encourage them into making the wrong move just so they could adjust to the taste of it.

So when I brought this first intern onto my team, I wanted

her to come into the position knowing and expecting failure, because through it she would grow. That one day she would fall down on her knees in failure and figure out how to pick herself up again. She would learn how to pick up other people with both arms.

When you're obsessing over perfection, your eyes can only ever be glued on the ground—fearful over each next step. When you look up, though, and throw back your shoulders, you start to realize we're all a little fearful and can all use more grace in the messiness of life. We can play a role that's different from being a terrorist on the internet who waits for someone to mess up. We can be the one who gets down on the floor next to the person who just took the fall and says, "Happens to the best of us. Need a hand?"

So that's what I started doing with my teammates, starting with that intern. I decided to write the kind of contract I wished I had signed when I first set out on my journey in adulthood. I drafted a contract that I hoped would make her proud to fail. Ready to fail.

I'm including it here for you. There's even a place for you to sign it. If you want to, you can rip it out of the book and hang it on your wall, where you'll see it regularly. Whatever you do, just promise me you'll fail.

"Promise Me You'll Fail" Contract

This is a big and bold promise to me that you will fail. Promise me you will stumble and make mistakes—big and little ones. Promise me you'll ask all your questions and take risks that feel bigger than you.

Promise me you won't let Fear drive the car. Or when you do let Fear drive the car, that you will eventually snap awake and say, "Wait, you don't have a license. Get out of the driver's seat," and you'll take back control. We all encounter Fear driving the vehicle at some point. It's a necessary, learned rhythm to keep taking back the keys. Promise me you won't wait for the day when Fear leaves completely, but you'll move forward, even when you are still scared.

Promise me you will explore the possibilities and partner with yourself instead of bullying your every movement. Promise me you will apply grace like sunscreen to the parts of you that you don't want to share with anyone else.

Promise to mess things up and try your best. Promise to give tasks everything you have in a moment when you're asked to give it all. Find peace with the doors that slam in your face over and over again. Give that rejection a sweet bear hug. Promise to cheer on the victories of others and not waste your time being sour over their accomplishments.

Promise me you won't let people belittle your creativity. Refuse to be kicked down by all the forces of the world that tell you, "You can't. You shouldn't. You won't." Silence the loud naysayers—the ones outside and on the inside of you—by one footstep at a time.

More than anything, just promise me you'll fail. Failure is one of the sweetest parts of being human. It molds you. It humbles you. It makes you new. And isn't that the hope? The only goal worth pinning your short life to? That you and I, at the end of all this, will come out looking new.

I, _____, promise to try, mess up, fail, and give myself and others grace as I go. Big, big grace.

NAME SIGNED: _____

DATE: _____

Chapter 10

Watch for Foxes

At some point, you'll lose yourself.

You'll lose yourself to work or parenthood. You'll lose yourself to school or a relationship. You'll lose yourself to an illness or a state of mind. If you realize this is part of it, that we get lost sometimes, then there will be more grace at the door when you finally come home to yourself.

We are living in a world where it's really easy to lose ourselves. The noise is loud. The distractions are endless. The number of things we can immerse ourselves in is limitless. Without realizing, you begin to scroll and idolize what you see on the screen. You begin to belittle where you currently are in life. You stop embracing this gift of life, and you lose yourself to what other people did before you or maybe did better than you.

Oswald Chambers writes about the "little foxes" mentioned in Solomon's Song of Songs in the Bible.[7] Solomon's readers of that time knew foxes to be destructive animals that would chew on the roots and stems of the vines and ruin the vineyards in bloom. "Is there anything competing for our strength in our devotion to the call of God?" Chambers writes. "It is not the devil, but the 'little foxes' that spoil the vines— the little annoyances, the little actual things that compete for our strength."[8]

I've turned this into a monthly question I can ask myself to gauge where I am on the map: What are the little foxes competing for my strength in right now?

When I know where the little foxes are, I can begin to change the narrative.

I felt parched, tired, and insecure leading into last year's season of Lent. My anxiety was running wild. I didn't feel like doing anything. I had lost motivation. I stopped wanting to make plans or see people because I was believing a lie that I was adding nothing to the lives of others.

Through a lot of prayer and seeking, God and I began to wade through the muck and get to the real reason I was so tired. Why I was feeling so weighed down. I noticed there was one thing that was zapping a good amount of energy from me.

Social media.

Every time I chose to access it, I felt more and more kicked down. It was making me tired. I am certain, knowing what I know now, that it was causing a lot of discontent in my heart. I hesitate to admit this because it sounds so trivial. Like, really? A social media app is causing you to feel drained? But I've clued into my dependency on it. Without even realizing it, I had begun to seek out affirmation and worth from a screen instead of asking God for it.

Of course, I was tired. I was expecting people to give me worth. I knew they couldn't, and I was still trying. I've known since the beginning of these platforms that people couldn't possibly fill the desire I have to be known and seen. I've preached people away from that posture. I've been a longtime advocate of not placing more value on social media than necessary. But then I found myself falling into the same rut and looking toward my phone for a soul feeding.

I noticed patterns I'd developed without even wanting to

develop them. I noticed that when I felt lonely or tired or insecure, I'd reach for my phone and begin to passively scroll. I say "passively" because I wasn't engaging with any content. I was using the content to size myself up, to put myself into a symbolic ranking of where I belonged and how much worth I possessed, based on other people. I was building a hierarchy, and I was almost always at the bottom of the hierarchy because that's what Fear will tell you when you become a listener to its messages: "You're no good. You don't add up."

I realize this is a grim picture to paint, but I also know other people—maybe you—feel it too. I think we've been caught in this vicious cycle of talking about social media and believing in the damage it can cause us but not being active in a new approach. We complain about it, but we indulge in it. We say we're going to quit it altogether, but we've developed addict-like behaviors that keep us from pulling away or striking some balance.

The great Saint Augustine believed that if our hearts were ever discontented, it simply meant we had gotten things out of order. We need to step back and rearrange some things, or as he says it, we must rightly order our loves.[9]

This was true in my life. I was putting things before God. I was putting things before the people I loved. I was putting too much of my energy into things that didn't even really matter.

So I made some changes.

And I am still making some changes.

I had to apply real limits to my life. I created a phone box where I now put my phone every morning. It sits on my shelf as a reminder that I can get good work done without needing to be always connected. I created time limits for apps, and I had Lane change my passcode so when the time runs out, I'm done for the day. I am locked out. I started writing letters again after a stretch of sending texts and emails. I began going for walks and calling friends on the phone just to hear their voices and ask them how they're doing. Each one of these micro-changes brings me back to what truly matters to me—living this life fully with all the energy I have.

What I had was a socially acceptable addiction because everyone else had their phones in their hands too.

There is a very famous TED Talk by a man named Johann Hari, who spent years trying to understand drug addiction. In his talk, he relayed an experiment conducted in the 1970s by Dr. Bruce Alexander. Dr. Alexander had already seen the outcome of experiments in the past where rats were put in a cage and given two water bottles to drink from—one water bottle filled with normal water, and another filled with drug water. Given the option, the rats always chose the drug water and died at rapid rates.

But Dr. Alexander wondered if it wasn't so much the water but the caged experience that caused the rats to move toward addiction. He decided to switch up the experiment by creating something called "Rat Park." In the rat park, the rats were given plenty of options—social opportunities, cheese, games to play, the works. He discovered that the social interactions and the community beat the drug water every time.

Hari finished his talk by saying, "The opposite of addiction is not sobriety; the opposite of addiction is connection."[10]

I think the same is true for our phones. We would put down our phones more and more if we had the chance to connect, really connect, face-to-face. But that kind of life is work. Good work and worthy work, but work that requires something of us.

These days, if I ever feel myself veering off the path again and losing myself, I repeat what a mentor once told me: do for one what you wish you could do for all.

This straightens me. It brings me back to the center. It reminds me that it isn't about all the people all over social media; it's about going back to the one you can help. When you want to worry about impact, remember a single person. If you start to become too consumed with people on a screen, shut off entirely and go love your husband. Or your best friend. Or your literal neighbor.

I cannot say the fire flooded back instantly as I made these small tweaks. That wouldn't be accurate. But from the dying fire came these embers. These small glimpses that passion and life were still there, that the story wasn't over. Something just needed to be stoked back to life. The story rewrites itself little by little, moment by moment.

Just the other night, Lane and I went bowling after dinner. Bowling isn't a thing we normally do, but we were both feeling competitive and not wanting the night to end. We played four games, and the most beautiful part was that I felt like we forged fresh memories. We did something more than the usual "sit on the couch and watch a show after dinner." We were present. We were cheering one another on. And I felt free, with the new boundaries I've laid down, to not pick up my phone and share our moments with the world.

That was the biggest thing I found missing from my life when I was wired to scroll—I was missing moments that were all mine, moments that weren't manufactured to be shared with the world for approval. With every outing, with every new adventure, we are gaining the moments back. I'm remembering the fire inside me that came from reading a book or going for a walk without my phone or getting lost in a project for hours. I remind myself that these are the embers I want to stoke.

It may feel daunting to begin again. Most of us feel like we have to have three hours to block off on our calendar if we want to make any sort of movement toward change. But as I worked to rewire my life so the fire could come back, I discovered the power that exists in just fifteen minutes.

Most of us have fifteen minutes. We say we don't, but we could find the space. We could put down the phone. We could watch less of that show. We could wake up a little earlier. You don't need a whole hour or a whole day; you just need to grab the tiny thread and start to pull.

Fifteen minutes to go for a walk. Fifteen minutes to meditate. Fifteen minutes to write some good sentences. At the start of the New Year, I had one primary goal: read more, scroll less. So I began that goal with fifteen minutes. I set a timer and picked up a book.

It was a small step in the right direction. It was a coming back to myself. And as I got into those pages, I remembered that I feel more alive when I'm reading a book. I feel more like myself. So I decided I was going to stoke the fire in me, fifteen minutes at a time. The number of minutes seems small, but any larger and I'd convince myself there just wasn't enough time.

If you're feeling like life has been knocked out of you, it may be time to look around and readjust. It may be time to cut some things out or build a better boundary. It may be time to have an honest conversation. It may be time to go to God with all the fears and the false idols you're grasping on to instead of him. You don't need to make big investments or buy fancy gadgets to come back to what you love. You just need to clear a little time to catch the little foxes standing in your way.

Don't believe for one second more the lie that you're not worth the time of recovery or that you cannot unearth the fire inside you again. It's still there. It hasn't gone out completely. There are embers, and where there are embers, there is a fire waiting to happen. Stoke those embers back to life.

Part 3

ROADBLOCKS + PLATEAUS

Encountering roadblocks isn't evidence that you're on the sidelines or God is absent.

Tough stuff is expected, and if we keep moving through it, it will produce in us a new level of endurance.

Chapter 11

Go into the Darkroom

I want to tell you an unfinished story because I believe in the power of stories still in development. I think God shows up most powerfully within the stories still unraveling and working themselves out.

Last year, I realized something was off in me. I didn't have words for it, and I couldn't name it, so I just called it "the no-name thing I couldn't explain if I tried." I was tired and mentally drained at all times. I'd been showing up to all of life's duties, but I wasn't living. I was simply existing, going through the motions of life and doing okay. Just okay.

Several months after that realization, with more of the same feelings, I was at a conference where one of the speakers talked about how we can ask God what is holding us back. It's as simple as that. We can flat-out ask him, and there's a pretty good chance he will answer. I say "pretty good chance" because I believe God always answers but not always according to our timelines. Sometimes we wait years for answers. Sometimes we don't see the answers this side of heaven.

"What is holding me back, God?" I asked it right then and there. "Why do I feel weighed down? Like I'm sleeping or something?"

I'm not exaggerating when I tell you the response was instantaneous. On this particular day, I heard something in my spirit snap back and say, "Discouragement. The spirit of discouragement is holding you back."

I scribbled it on a piece of paper and thought about it the whole day until I was able to get a moment alone. Staring down at that word, I began to doubt what I had heard. The spirit of discouragement? Is that even a thing?

I put those three words into Google, and the results shocked me.

In my research, I discovered this definition for *discouragement*: "The verb to *discourage* means 'to deprive of confidence, hope or spirit; dishearten, daunt.' *Afflict, beat down, demoralize, depress, dismay, distress, frighten, intimidate, irk,* and *trouble* are synonyms of the word *discourage*."[11]

This was it. These were the exact feelings. I felt mildly depressed. I felt beaten down. I felt like I was frightened to make the next move. I wanted to shrink away from every life obligation, put on a wig, and hightail it away from all present responsibilities.

And what was strange is that I had no evidence of anything around me that should have been beating me down or causing me to lose hope.

Now that I've spent more time researching this "discouragement," I no longer think something needs to happen to trigger the feeling coming on like an onslaught. I think it can just walk through the door one day when you're not looking, duffel bag in hand and, slowly but surely, begin to unpack its things. A shirt here. A pair of pants there. Before long, discouragement has moved in entirely and become an attitude. A posture. It has eaten all your food and left you starved. It has given commentary on your life, and you've believed it. It has shown up with a single color in its wardrobe—gray—and it has proceeded to cloak you in that gray mess.

I think we can take the word *discouragement,* omit it from all the sentences I just wrote, and fill in the blank with any feeling we're currently grappling with. Anger. Envy. Laziness. Idleness. Comparison. All of these things, no matter what names we think to give them, show up to steal away our lives without mercy.

They are the opposite of abundance. They are soul-sucking and are the things that make it a fight to keep our faith as we grow older. We need to realize there is a force, a very real force, that wants us to have no faith at all, and so it will show up in any form or fashion necessary to trip us, stop us, break us down, and leave us lifeless.

After figuring out that discouragement was, indeed, the thing holding me back, I didn't do anything with it beyond telling other people what I'd heard.

I went around to anyone who would listen and told them, with genuine enthusiasm, "I've been in a pit, and God revealed to me what has been holding me back. It's the spirit of discouragement! That's what it is."

But identifying the roadblock doesn't mean you've gotten over it or found a way to work your way through it. I'd had the revelation. I knew now what the roadblock was. But it sat there. And nothing on the inside changed for a long while. I confused getting the revelation with going through the transformation.

I went on thinking for the next five months that just having the revelation was enough. It would be like you were holding on to a travel brochure for a place you desperately wanted to visit but never saved the pennies and didn't book the trip—you just held tightly to the brochure, thinking, *This is enough. This is enough to look at the pictures and just imagine my being there.*

Just because God gave you a revelation doesn't mean you've walked through the transformation.

In February of this last year, five months after the revelation, the real work began—the real "I am going to face this discouragement and handle it until it's no longer an issue" work. This work involved being relentless in going back to God. I physically cleared space for him as a representation that I was ready to make room for whatever he wanted to do. I was handing over the keys. I was done with my own methods of self-help.

I cleaned out the little closet in my office that I had used for storage and Christmas decorations and turned it into a prayer closet. Daily, I would make myself enter the little closet without my phone or any distractions, and I would sit there and pray. I did this every day for forty days, writing down my prayers on printer paper and covering my walls with them. I had to be relentless in making this space each day to meet with God. Even if I didn't yet feel like it was the most important thing on my calendar, I protected it and blocked it off until the feelings of necessity became real.

At the time this was all happening, I was also wrapped up in a show on Netflix called *Tidying Up with Marie Kondo*. It was genius on Netflix's part to release this show at the start of January, when everyone wants to be a new person and finally fold their clothes and get their act together.

The star of the show is a woman named Marie Kondo, who enters the houses of people who need more space. They are drowning in stuff. With her kind demeanor and sweet spirit, she helps each family become free. But she always starts with the bedroom. There she will ask the individual to take all of their stuff out of the drawers and closets and put it in a pile on the bed.

I listened to her. As I watched episodes on my computer, I pulled out every ounce of clothing and made a massive pile on the bed. I did everything she told me to do. I left no socks, no hats, no accessories behind. And then, item by item, I was instructed to deal with it. Now I'll admit, it was a little strange to hold up a piece of clothing and ask myself the question, "Does this give me joy?"

But I found myself getting really into the process. And it pulled me into a space of introspection as I wondered about the correlation this may have to the stuff we keep in our brains and things we try to hide from others and the rest of the world. And it even inspired me during my "junk hour" with God to ask these questions: *What would it look like to take this same approach with internal thoughts, beliefs, and the messages I tell myself? What if I just hauled it all out into the light—no matter how good, bad, or ugly it seemed—and forced myself to deal with it?*

The big stuff—the stuff that acts as a roadblock between you and who you want to become—is not the sort of stuff you can deal with once and never wrestle with again. It takes time. It takes patience and lots of packets of grace. It's the kind of stuff you must haul out into the light daily so it doesn't get the chance to blend in with the walls of your heart and steal from the better stories you are meant to live.

God is kind. He isn't standing in the center of your issues with his arms crossed and a look of disdain on his face. He does not shame us, and so if you ever feel the shame seeping into the corners of your heart, you need to know that isn't him.

If you think God is looking at you like you're "less than," I want you to grab really tightly to what I'm about to tell you. The encouragement comes from the prophet Isaiah. God tells his people, "I publicly proclaim bold promises. I do not whisper obscurities in some dark corner."[12] He's not a God of confusion. He isn't trying to derail you. He isn't here to confuse you or make you mess up or leave you hopeless.

When you hear shame like a familiar voice speaking in the background of your heart, take the liberty to remind yourself, *God does not whisper weird things that don't make sense. That is not him. That is not his character. My God speaks in promises. His language is laced with promises, and he is not here to shame me.*

This is what I mean by the "unfinished story": I am still in the midst of mine. I am still having to show up and work alongside God daily. It is hard work, and it's a fight, but I've decided that I do not want discouragement to keep showing up with suitcases to unpack his gray capsule wardrobe. So I show up to fight. And God shows up to fight. And I keep showing up. And he keeps showing up. And on days when I cannot, he can. And days when I can, he can times two. And I believe and remember the taste of freedom. And I hold on to the promises I've held close to my chest. And I keep going, knowing that my God is a fighter, and freedom will not be a footnote in my story.

The thing is, I'm seeing some remarkable results from dealing with this discouragement and not shoving it away because I'm sick of looking at it. But if you had asked me months ago, I would have told you I didn't want discouragement to be the vehicle that drove me toward these remarkable results. I would have wanted something simpler, or maybe something I'd already dealt with in the past so I could identify that path out of it more quickly. I would have asked God for a list of possible roadblocks so I could pick the best one for my calendar. Oswald Chambers would be the first to tell you it doesn't work that way: "God can never make us into wine if we object to the fingers He chooses to use to crush us."[13] We cannot become the best versions of ourselves if we keep saying no to the roadblocks God has allowed in our lives so we can learn how to make our way through them.

Maybe you're in the middle of dealing with your roadblock

right now, and you're tired. You're over it. You keep thinking to yourself, *I don't have what it takes to go any farther.* But hope isn't lost. Hope didn't find the back exit. It may seem bleak. It may seem hard. But God knew you could be in this fight, and he knew the outcome of the fight before you stepped in.

The results of going into the darkroom, going wherever God leads you, is necessary and golden. Don't stop at the revelation. Go on through until you reach the transformation. He has plans for the person you are becoming. I have so much faith that this is true for you.

I just keep getting this picture in my mind of a Polaroid camera every time I think of this story, of how we are developing through the roadblocks. I hear the snap, click, and churn of the little camera processing and spitting out a blank, white piece of film. The picture isn't there just yet. It's coming though . . . It's coming.

But it needs some time and some light to develop. You can shake it if you want to, but it doesn't make the process go any faster (at least I don't think it does). You'll just have to wait. And keep looking for that image to fully appear. But it's coming. It's definitely coming.

Chapter 12

Count the Ravens

I have an app on my phone that I use for running. I'm someone who has always wanted to be a runner and who likes the high that comes from running a few good miles but I've never been able to get myself fully into a sustainable rhythm.

The running app talks to me. I can select a series of different runs where someone will give me pep talks and remind me why I began running in the first place. My friends tell me they would hate this, that they're more "music people," but I am in my element when someone is speaking into my ear and telling me not to quit. I like it when a positive voice can combat the inner critic in my head.

There's a coach in my app named Adam, and he takes my mind off my heavy breathing and the sound of my shoes pounding the pavement. One day, Adam tells me we are building my endurance. With every run and every additional mile, we are stretching my capacity.

The thing is, endurance isn't what I thought it was all these years. When I picture endurance, I think about being the best. I thought it meant ruling the day or being the last one standing. I associate endurance with top athletes, with the ones who win the races. But that's not what endurance means. The definition of endurance, as Adam the running coach informs me, is "to remain in existence."

To remain in existence. That's the real meaning.

To continue or last. To not melt into the darkness. To not give up on the fight. To keep going, even if it means the only thing you might do today is get out of bed and put on some shoes. Some days the victory is the shoes; other days, it's the pants.

Where I thought endurance meant you outlasted everyone, I got it all wrong. Endurance means you go on living. You experience hard days, days that don't go as you planned them to, but you know in your core that the fight is not over for good. You go to sleep. You lay your tired head down. You wake up. And you try again. This is endurance—trying again, against all odds.

It wasn't until I experienced depression that I realized the whole "just be stronger" and "wake up and rule the day" mentality doesn't always work. It doesn't mean you have to bow down to your circumstances or forge an identity out of your weakness, but it does mean that there will be a lot of days that don't feel as empowering as a Nike commercial. There will be plenty of days when you "just do it" and feel nothing at all. And then there will be other days for naps and grace and the courage to just say, "We will try this all again tomorrow."

Some days you may wake up, and though there seems to be nothing wrong, anxiety will be knotted in your chest. Some days you will wake up to darkness—it will be waiting there at the foot of your bed, eagerly anticipating when you'll try to rise—and it will follow you throughout the day. It will hover.

I don't say this to discourage you or to make you want to give up. I share it to be honest that some days feel like the darkness is winning, and yet you must know that the darkness cannot have the final word in your life.

When the whole world sounds like a drill sergeant making you feel like you need to do more, produce more, eat less, burn more, try harder, and speak louder, it's okay to clear out the noise and just be. Just be. It's okay to do what you can and stack up the small victories—what personally feels big to you—at the end of a long day. It's okay to be tired. It's okay to feel a little lost. These kinds of days matter too.

Sometimes when you're in a slump, it's going to be hard to "find God." You won't feel him.

I'm learning it's usually when our surroundings don't look like we want them to look that we begin to think God is slacking on our stories.

It was when I reached a point of the honeymoon period being over in my move to Atlanta and the thrill of something new faded away that I stopped thinking God was at work. I went from regarding him as the God who was always there and always constant and always kind to seeing him as the God with spotty cell phone service and a tendency to ghost for days at a time.

But it was there, in the moments when I couldn't "find" God, that I realized he wasn't being absent; he was simply teaching me to understand him in a new way. If God existed in my brain only when times were good or going my way, that's a pretty small God. That's too small of a story line. There had to be something more to it than that. I was going to have to fight to discover a God who cared about my feelings but wasn't dependent on my feelings to prove himself.

Paul David Tripp writes in his book *Suffering*, "Suffering has the power to expose what you have been trusting all along. If you lose your hope when your physical body fails, maybe your hope wasn't really in your Savior after all."[14] In his journey through physical illness, he realized that much of his faith in God was just self-reliance—a confidence based on his own abilities that he could not recognize until he was unable to do anything but simply remain in existence and depend on something bigger than himself.

I think we would rather skip the parts of the story where God feels absent or where our bodies are riddled with illness or where our brains don't feel like our own, but I think God uses the winters and the dark nights to do something he cannot do when everything is good and fine and beautiful. He has our attention. He's on the move.

Think about the Old Testament character Elijah. Elijah was, simply put, a force. He knew God was God and that all the stories about God were true, and he could not keep quiet about it. What I love most about Elijah is that he expected miracles. He didn't get trapped in small ways of thinking or lose the wonder of God, like I so often do. He woke up expectant, ready for God to be big and real in the lives of others.

At one point, God asks Elijah to confront a king who is doing some despicable things. The king is doing what most of the kings did at that time—forgetting God and choosing to worship lower-case "g" gods. Of all the things God hates, this is a biggie, and it's a huge struggle of humanity: to keep our eyes on God and not worship other gods.

After Elijah tells the king he's going to be in deep trouble and a drought spreads out over the land, God tells Elijah he needs to run and hide. Fast, because he is being hunted. He instructs Elijah to hide out by a brook—there he'll have water to drink, and ravens will come and feed him daily.[15]

When I first read this, I thought, *Oh cute, ravens are going to feed him*. But we should know that ravens at that time were considered among the most despicable of all the creatures. God could have sent a dove or a Harry Potter owl, but he sent a raven. He used one of the most unlikely things to deliver his daily provisions.

God is in the business of using the most unexpected elements to make himself known. I had to learn this in my own story when people I thought were going to show up for me didn't. They were nowhere to be found. They were either turned off or scared off by the rawness of the depression, and I get it. I wasn't angry. I understood, because suffering isn't pretty to look at. But where the void was felt, others arrived. Unexpected people—people I would have never guessed would be the ones who checked in on me, held me up, or laid their hands on me to pray.

Turns out, God didn't want to use my map to bring about my healing. He had detours he wanted us to take. He had people he wanted to introduce into the story—people I would have never paid attention to if everything in life had been going just fine. He had the most unlikely people and things ready to come and find me.

Maybe that's you right now. Your knees are on the bathroom floor. You feel like you've come to the end of yourself. You can no longer muster up the strength and just get better. Here's what I am begging you to do: Tell someone about it. Be honest with them. Don't let shame or fear of what someone might think keep you from being honest about where you are on the map. We cannot expect people to show up for us if we don't first tell them we are in need.

After you let someone in, remember this moment. Take a mental picture of it. Remember the view. You won't be in this place forever.

Because here's the thing about God and pain: He never plans to leave you just as you are. You're far too precious to him to not upgrade you, to swap out parts of you for a newer model. When you know stories about the dark, you become a light to others. You get to show the way. You get to sit on the floor with people or on the other end of the phone, not saying a word because you know words can't change the present pain. You get to help others just be, as you decide to just be with them.

New songs are born with your knees on the bathroom floor all the time. New songs are born as you put your hands on the floor and prop yourself up, shaking as you stand. And nothing, nothing feels more glorious and life-giving than the moment you discover you're standing for the first time in what seems like a very long while.

You may not see it right now, but something bigger is happening. Something is hatching in your spirit, and it's the kind of thing that won't soon go away. It's a new room, a new part of you. And from now on, you're going to be able to take people there, and you'll have new strength to sit with them in their empty times. You are going to finally understand. You are going to be one of the unlikely who show up for someone else's rock-bottom raven time.

During those times when it feels like all you're doing is remaining in existence, I know how easily the fear can sweep in and tell you you're making no progress and that God isn't here.

In those times when the fear wants to plug up your ears, count the ravens. If you only have the strength to do one thing, do this: Begin counting the ravens. That's all. Whether you see it or not, God is showing up. He is doing things around you— things that may not look the way you wanted them to look. They may not feel the way you wanted them to feel. But there are ravens, circling the sky to bring you provision. Train your eyes to see them. Train your eyes to look for them, and count them daily. Every single day, there will be a new provision.

It's okay if you can't stand up on your feet and shout with joy, but I would tell you to pull out a notebook and scribble down the ravens you see with each new day—the unlikely ways God is showing up for you. I feel pretty strongly about this part—about writing this down instead of trying to keep it all in your mind. We forget too easily. We move on too quickly. When you write something down, you solidify it. You give yourself something to go back to, something to remember when the darkness gets thicker. When you declare goodness and the evidence of God moving in the midst of the pain and suffering, you forge a fight song in the wilderness that cannot be taken away from you. You become someone who offers thanksgiving to God when the world expects you to grumble and give up.

You'll be amazed as you start to see the ravens showing up, day after day, with the most unexpected forms of provision. People you haven't talked to in years. Cups of tea. Friends who pray. The taste of food after you've spent a long time not tasting anything at all. A full night of sleep. A good therapy session. These are the things that strung me back together when I was in the darkest places. I stopped needing to be completely out of the woods and just realized that God is here. He is providing. He is teaching me to depend on him.

A walk around the neighborhood. A fresh autumn breeze. Blankets and good company. Clarity. A church service that speaks deeply and powerfully after a long drought. All of these things are ravens flying through the dark to provide for you.

One day, you'll want to remember these things. The cracks in the ceiling where the light poured through. One day, these ravens will be evidence that you came through the long woods and walked out better than before.

One day, because of what you've seen with your own two eyes, you'll be able to grab the hand of someone else, squeeze it tight, and say, "Count the ravens. Whether you believe it or not, God is here."

Chapter 13

Lay Down the Arrows

Here's the thing they don't teach you in high school or college: Feelings left unmonitored will not just go away. They won't get bored and leave. Feelings that you attempt to skip over or shove down will find a way to plant some mean roots in your heart. They will do their very best to make you mad about other things—other people, your job, traffic jams, plans, expectations. They will multiply.

I'm on a prayer team at my church. A few dozen women get together every month to pray for those who will be attending a monthly women's gathering in our space. Before the event, we split up and walk the entire auditorium, praying over all the seats.

I imagine some people are really good and holy when it comes to this job, and they have no problem pouring out their hearts to God. I run out of things to say sometimes, so when I finish praying for other people, I naturally slide into this sort of heart-to-heart with God where I tell him all the things I've been holding back on.

On this particular night, I was dealing with a lot of frustration and bitterness. They were ugly feelings that I wanted more than anything to get rid of, but they kept sprouting up and taking me down.

I was hurting, and I was upset with one person in my life. I didn't even have anything to be hurt or upset over anymore.

Forgiveness words had been said and done and repeated for good measure, but I was still mad.

My feelings were telling me, *Stay down. Stay sad. Stay angry. Stay bitter. Don't let it go. Don't move on. Don't forgive. Just live in this space. Just pitch a tent in these woods and get comfortable.*

As I weaved through the aisles of the church, I kept asking God, "What am I missing? What am I missing? What am I not seeing? Why won't this anger just leave?"

Moments later, I saw this picture in my brain. I was standing in this same auditorium, except all the chairs were gone. I had a quiver full of arrows on my back. As I pulled each arrow out, I realized its tip would flame up as I aimed at a target across the room. I was mercilessly pulling back and shooting these arrows at the target, over and over and over again. I was hitting the target every time. And then I turned my head, and I realized there was another target, one I hadn't even thought to aim for.

"You're shooting arrows at the wrong target," I said underneath my breath.

"You're mad at the wrong thing. You're stuck, and you cannot move forward until you stop shooting your arrows at this target. You're thinking that if. you. just. keep. shooting. then eventually something will break. But what if the battle is already over?"

There was a deep pit of resentment in me, a part of me that thought I deserved my anger. I should have my bitterness. I should get to keep shooting my flaming arrows at the target. And the reality was that I could keep my anger. I could hold on to it for a long time. But I knew in that moment that I wasn't aiming for the right target, that holding on to my anger would only hold me back from walking into the freedom God had for me.

Imagine this. Once upon a time, anger built a house for you. Resentment helped erect the roof. Bitterness put in the tiles. They built this house for you, and they intended for you to stay in it. Grow old in it. Come back to it day after day.

And then one day, you smartened up and realized that you don't have to stay in that house anymore. You could pack up the boxes and the bins and get out of there. Turns out, nothing was stopping you.

So you do it. You pack up the things. You tape up the boxes. You leave behind your key. And you move somewhere new. Somewhere spacious. Somewhere good. And you feel like you can maybe breathe again for the first time in a while.

Just as you grow comfortable in this new space, something happens to remind you of what you left. That house. That place you grew so comfortable with. The house you know by heart— the house that anger built for you.

So one day, you get up and get dressed. You put on your running shoes. You jog over to that old house. And you just stay there for a while. You look through the windows. You check to see if you can get inside. You spend time there, and then you decide to come back the next day. Over and over again, you go back to that familiar house.

You don't live there anymore. Your furniture is gone. And yet nothing and no one but yourself can stop you from putting on your running shoes and going back to the place that used to hold you hostage. That's on you. You have to be the one to move forward. To get braver. To let go. To move on. To say no when the anger tempts you to say unkind things about someone you love.

Take advice from someone who is all too comfortable with going back to visit houses she no longer lives in anymore: Eventually, you have to be so fed up with holding yourself back that you finally, finally walk into new territory. At one point or another, you've got to be brave and strong enough to say,

"I'm done. The war is over. There's nothing to fight anymore. There's no target to shoot at. I'm choosing to let go. I'm not going back to that house anymore."

Letting go may not happen overnight. You may have to apply these feelings of love and forgiveness and hope several times a day. Forgiveness is like sunscreen—you have to reapply it every eighty minutes. But you get a choice. Every single day you get to choose—old feelings that don't deserve your energy or feelings of love and gratitude. Hope and peace.

I wrote that last paragraph so easily. It practically spilled out of me, and I laughed when I saw it there on the page, as if choosing better feelings is simple. Actually, for a long time, you're probably going to feel like a little child who doesn't know how to stop picking that thing up. You will scold yourself. You may yell at yourself. Reapply the grace, once again, and give yourself credit for where you're standing. Chances are, you're a little farther down the road than you were yesterday.

The reality in my own story is, that evening, the one with the prayer and arrows, wasn't the last time I was angry. I still get angry sometimes over the same situation, but I step back and remind myself, *Hey, we are not going back to that place anymore.* And then I say to God, "Here, God. You can hold on to this thing because I don't want to hold on to it. And I am not going to bother apologizing profusely for the fact that I've handed you this thing fifty-six times before. I'm going for number fifty-seven. I might be back tomorrow to pick it up again, but let's hope fifty-seven is the time things stick."

God isn't exasperated if this is the fifty-seventh time you've had to let "this thing" go. He's more like, "Fifty-seven? Good job. Righteous effort! I'll see you at fifty-eight, babycakes."

And then after I let the feeling go for the fifty-seventh time,

I do something I honestly cannot take credit for. I learned it during the year I basically memorized *Eat, Pray, Love* as I ate and prayed and loved my way through my first heavy heartbreak—the first heartbreak that ever took something from me.

There's a part in the book where Liz, who is the main character, is having a conversation with a man named Richard from Texas. In the conversation, she complains about how her heart is broken and how she cannot seem to move on from that man who broke her heart. She wanted to hold on just a little longer because, underneath all the other feelings, she missed him.

And then Richard from Texas says the most profound thing in the world: "Send him some love and light every time you think about him, and then drop it."[16] So this is what I do now every time the anger or the pain tries to make me run back to the house I don't live in anymore, the one that used to control me. I stop and deliberately think about the person who hurt me. I imagine them standing there when this sudden rush of light and love come pouring in. I picture them living a good and happy life. I think of them throwing their head back and laughing.

As good ole Richard recommends, I send them away with a blessing, and then I let it go. I take that next step forward because freedom isn't reserved for other people who have it more together than me. Freedom is waiting, and when I release my hands from the anger and pain that I've been white-knuckling for so long, I suddenly realize I can grab that freedom with two hands.

Chapter 14

Evict the Envy

There was an entire summer a few years back when I lived at the foot of Mount Galatians—camped out in the five chapters of that book until I could nearly recite the words by heart.

When I study the Bible, I like to bounce around and explore different things, but sometimes God has me camp out somewhere in the Bible for longer than I'd prefer. No matter how much I try to move somewhere else, I feel this pull to stay right where I'm at. This "camping out" can last a few days or a few weeks.

The book of Galatians, if you get up close, is a book about freedom. Freedom is the essence of the gospel story, yet it's often the first thing we forget we've been given. Paul originally spent some time with the churches in the province of Galatia. He introduced them to that sweet freedom. They devoured it. They bought in. But he found out later that they picked up legalism. They forgot all about the freedom and retreated back to their old ways. And Paul was wrecked by that. Paul was sick over what was going on, and he wanted to win those people back to God.

I remember reading a verse at the beginning of that "Summer of Galatians" in which Paul says to the people, "You were running a good race. Who cut in on you to keep you from obeying the truth?"[17]

At that moment, some legitimate ugly crying ensued. I could

see myself on the sidelines, feeling like I was helpless to get back into the race. I could see myself being benched by my own issues and wondering why it was so hard to just start again. And then God comes walking up to me, bending down to ask, "What happened? You were doing so well. What got into you?"

I knew exactly what it was that kept me from running the race that summer. It was Envy. Envy keeps a lot of us from staying in our lane and making an impact.

Envy and jealousy are not the same things. Jealousy is a form of possessiveness while envy is a sense of wanting what someone else has. Envy is a bucktooth cousin of the Fear family. He's sitting there in that Fear family photo, wearing a wool turtleneck and a righteous comb-over.

I knew my envy was rooted in the fear that good stuff would happen for other people but not for me. My envy was rooted in the belief that God was for other people but had a distaste when it came to me. These lies had started small and subtle, but I gave them room to spread out and grow until they overtook me, as was their plan all along.

On the outside, I was peddling hope to everyone around me, but I didn't believe it for myself. I was sick with fear daily, and there was no joy. My husband can attest to the little eyedropper amounts of joy I experienced.

The fear got worse. I started comparing myself to other people, with Envy in my side pocket. I measured people. Based on my own success, I measured whether or not I was further ahead or behind them. If I had more than they did, I was doing okay. If I had less than they did—less popularity, fewer awards, fewer accomplishments—my entire day would crumble. I would be stuck in my feelings, helpless to move forward because my worth was based on other people. They were my barometer for success. They were who I looked to to see how I was doing, and the whole process was miserable.

I know this time in my life served a purpose, but I will always look back on it with a bit of remorse because I felt little to no freedom my first year of marriage. I regressed hard. One of the traits that Lane fell in love with was my ability to be confident and sure of what God had for me. And that was the first thing that slipped out the back door when I let the fear come and take over.

Envy plundered so much from me. It tainted my vision and gave me a sort of tunnel vision for the things I didn't have. And when you've got that kind of tunnel vision, it becomes extremely hard to be grateful for what you do have. For how far you've come or how much you've fought. There is that little crooked voice of Envy in the background, saying, "Why even work so hard? All that hard work, and someone managed to go out there and do it ten times better than you."

There will always be someone prettier than us or more popular than us. There will always be someone with more notoriety than us or more charisma than us. There will always be someone who looks like they have it all together when you're just trying to get through the day without spilling coffee on your shirt for a second time. If we're not careful, we will become imprisoned by the act of comparing our lives to the lives of other people, and it will never serve us anything other than strife. But there is a better path. There is a better way, and I can confidently tell you that I've walked the path. I know it exists.

Judith Orloff, the author of *Emotional Freedom*, writes this about envy: "It's difficult to admit, to ourselves or others, that we don't want the best for others because their attributes, assets, or accomplishments make us feel small . . . Nevertheless, to be free, we must do both."[18]

To be free, we must do both.

To be honest, this has been a really hard area of my life to talk about. I'm one of the most honest talkers, and I carry little to no shame about airing what I'm currently going through, but I've realized that as I did this little dance with Envy, it's not something any of us readily admit. It's not as packaged an issue as low self-esteem or perfectionism. At the root of envy, there is a belief that you don't want the best for other people, and I feel like that's a little too ugly to admit to someone over coffee. Because of that, we suffer in silence for longer than is necessary. We get open and honest with people about other hindrances, but we ignore this roadblock that, if we could just get past it, might change nearly everything.

I will tell you the only thing that worked for me—the only journey God led me on to become truly, truly free from the envy—didn't involve my sitting in a room and thinking about myself until I uncovered all the problems and prayed through every area. Quite the opposite. I only found the freedom I'd so badly wanted to taste for years when I stopped trusting every feeling I encountered and put into the forefront the very people I was measuring and asked myself a better question: How can I help them run better?

That's what Paul talks about when he mentions freedom in his letter to the churches in Galatia. He tells the believers that the only way to make their freedom multiply is to "serve one another humbly in love."[19] That is how freedom grows.

How can I cheer them on? How can I be excited for them? How can I show I care? I'm finding that the feeling of envy is almost always completely separate from what I think about the person I'm feeling envious of. At my core, I truly like them. They're really cool. They're doing good and beautiful work.

But Envy wants to seep into me with a ballad that just isn't true—a ballad that they belong in the story but not me.

The results of forcing ourselves out of introspection and into the lives of other people to be a source of light and love change everything. I used to be skeptical of that, and now I live by it. The only way I broke free of the grips of Envy was through breaking the ballad by pulling out the poster board, making the glittery sign, and learning to cheer louder than anyone else.

I don't want you to lose the most precious people because of envy, because of a feeling that seeps in when they "get" what you wanted.

Someone recently emailed me and told me she was having the hardest time celebrating her friend because she was envious of her. Her friend was getting married, and she felt left behind, like everyone had found their person and she was still waiting. She went on to tell me she could not do a single thing for her friend because she was too busy being entangled in hatred and bitterness. She was too busy attending her own pity party that she was forgetting to show up to her friend's celebration of something really sweet and wonderful.

Even though the actions feel a little forced at first, the only remedy I've found thus far for envy is choosing to become active in love. The more you show up to love, the more you tell Envy and its cohorts that they can no longer occupy the space you've given them in the past. The lease is up. There is no renewal. You will not become one of those people who hates it when other people experience victory. If you want to send Envy a true eviction notice, then daily choose celebration over comparison until it becomes a natural posture.

I ended up telling this girl what I'd begrudgingly tell myself: "Celebrate your friend, even if you don't feel like it. Go to Target right this moment and buy a card. Buy a gift if you can. Write the kindest and most encouraging message you can write. You may need a prayer session before you get the words out there, but God will gladly give you encouraging words to borrow. Deep down, under all the ugly feelings you don't understand, you love this friend and you want to see her win. The hard truth is that her celebration has nothing to do with you, just as on the biggest day of your life, it will have nothing to do with her, but you'd still hope she'd show up for it. I'm afraid, if you allow it to, that the fear will try to make you distant from the people who really need your rally cries and celebration chants today. Ultimately, you get to choose. You get to choose whether you're going to love your friend well or whether you'll walk away from her, talk behind her back, or secretly wish bad on her while she walks through a really exciting time in life. Would you want her to stand by you and celebrate you?"

Just keep breaking the fear with love. That's all I think we can do. Even when the fear shows up with a stronger posse, harassing you and trying to force you back into a mold that you're too strong for now, keep learning how to fight this hard battle with love.

In the battle between love and fear, love always has the power to win. But love must be trained. We need to learn to train it for the fight.

Chapter 15

Stand Still

In the trenches of Craigslist, beyond the ads for free couches or free roommates, is a space called Missed Connections. It's where all the romantics go to spend their evenings when they can't sleep and want to believe the world is still beautiful when the news is so dark. At least that's one of my coping mechanisms.

You could consider this place a digital town square where people post about the "missed connections" they've encountered while going about their days. That cute guy they saw in the coffee shop but never mustered up the courage to say hello to. That girl in the floral dress and Chucks who passed you in the grocery store. I'll admit the ads are more romantic in a city like New York than in Atlanta, where the missed connection posts read less like poetry and more like people who are one step away from having an AMBER alert put out on them.

A few years ago, a Missed Connections ad that was posted in the Boston page went viral. The headline of the ad read, "I met you in the rain on the last night of 1972." The letter was written by a man who served in the Vietnam War. He came home to Massachusetts, haunted by all the terrible things he had seen and done, and decided he'd take his own life on the last day of the year.

He headed outside to take one last walk around his city of Boston before going home to a bottle of whiskey and a gun.

Midway through his walk, it began to rain. As he rounded back to his apartment, he saw her. A woman in a bright teal dress was taking shelter beneath the balcony of the Old State House. He'd never seen anything as beautiful as her. As he moved closer to join her under the balcony, he noticed she'd been crying. He offered to get her a cup of coffee. The woman led him down to the avenue to Neisner's, a popular five and dime at the time.

After an hour or so of talking, the man headed for the bathroom. I can imagine his head was spinning with more things he wanted to tell, stories he wanted to make sure to share. When he walked back toward the counter where the two of them had been sitting, the woman was gone. Nothing was left in her place. No phone number, no way to reach her. It was as if he'd been drinking coffee with a ghost that whole time.

The man writes that for the next year of his life, he went back to that diner, looking for the girl in the teal gown, but he never saw her again.

The man's obsession with finding her eventually swallowed up his desire to end his own life. In a way, she gave him a new purpose. She woke him up and reminded him to keep searching through the pain. The woman in the teal dress saved him.

But still, he never saw her again. Time passed. He met someone else. He married and had children. I bet he still felt a lump in his throat every time he passed that diner though.

In the ad, the man writes to tell the woman—wherever she is—that he lived a full life. He did. He signed the note by saying, "So wherever you've been, wherever you are, and wherever you're going, know this: you are with me still."

At the time I first read that, I felt like it related to the juncture I'd recently been at with God—one of those periods when you feel like God is absent. Like, he was with me up until a certain point, and then he ran for the door the second I turned around. I had no idea this juncture in my faith wasn't an indication that my faith would become smaller; it was an invitation for God to be bigger.

But still, I thought for so long that I was like the man in the coffee shop who felt abandoned by God. I pictured myself going back there day after day but still not feeling like God was meeting me where I was at. I had so many moments of thinking, *Where are you in all of this? Where did you go?*

And then one day, after I walked through some darkness and found myself on the other side of the storm clouds that were clearing, the story flipped. I was no longer the man in the coffee shop waiting for God to come back. Suddenly I was the woman in the teal ball gown. The one who chose to run. I got the story all wrong, but I wouldn't see it until I became confident that God is not a runner. *Abandonment* is not a word in his vocabulary.

My inbox is full of people who think that God fled in the middle of the night, and I don't always know what to tell people to give them hope because I know that feeling and it feels so real. But I knew I had to bring it up because we're talking about "fighting," and there's a tendency when we adopt this fight talk and lace together these empowering anthems for ourselves to forget about God. We make it a "me" story, and we rely heavily on our own inner strength, not realizing it has become our mini savior.

On the day where the darkness arrives or it feels like the fog will never clear, Fear will try to tell you you're all alone and it's up to you to get better, to be stronger, and to fight your way out. When this day comes, sing into yourself a different story: I am not alone. I am not fighting this battle alone. God is here. I'm okay.

When your fight songs run out, God will take over.

This is truth. It's written right in the Bible: "The LORD will fight for you; you need only to be still."[20]

But those words seem so hard. They seem so countercultural. What does it even look like to be still? I want to fight and move and push and pummel and make traction and cross things off lists.

Yet sometimes victory is sitting still when your heart is broken and you cannot find the words, trusting that God knows how to fight for you in realms you cannot see with your own two eyes.

Sometimes victory is saying, "God, I have no strength to do this day. Help me to go through the motions, and please fight for me because I just can't do it on my own."

Sometimes victory is being okay with the to-do list not working and the groceries not being ordered on time and the whole "system" you've created going off-kilter, and with asking God to give you hope, to show up in the lifeboat because you are sinking fast.

I know God provides this hope. I've seen the miracles. I know how the story ends for the weak and weary.

There's this little practice we can engage in when it feels like all hope is lost. It's waiting in Psalm 42. For years I thought Psalm 42 was just a depressing psalm written by an overdramatic dude who could only cry out, "Where are you, God?" And then I grew up and realized those times are very real. As I did research about the psalm, I discovered it is not a collection of dramatic words; it's considered to be what scholars call an "instructional song." It's meant to be a road map for those who feel like God is absent. It is packed with actions we can take—things we can hum to ourselves—when it feels like all hope exited the diner while we were in the restroom.

The psalmist says at one point, "When my soul is in the dumps, I rehearse everything I know of you."[21]

Sometimes when you have no strength to pray and cannot figure out what to do in the struggle, you can go into rehearsal mode. You can go back and back and back to find God in the archives of your life.

This is why I keep all of my old journals in my closet. I keep them there for the days when I need to be reminded of who God was in the past so I can know he is still that same God for this day. There's no right or wrong way to rehearse. I simply grab a stack of journals and a spot on my big chair, and I begin to read the past miracles I've seen and written down until I remember that God hasn't left and that he has answered in the past. I can look at the prayers I highlighted and circled—thinking to myself at the time there was no way there'd be an answer—and I can see how God showed up at every juncture, even when I forgot to ask him to be there.

This is why I am a notetaker. This is why I keep the notebooks and flag the pages in my Bible and have printer paper hung up all over my walls instead of classy artwork. I like to be surrounded by reminders—reminders that I am not fighting alone. Reminders that God is big when I feel small. Reminders that I don't have to hold the world together. I can just stand still, and he will show up for me.

And if right now you aren't experiencing a drought or a dark patch of woods, then this could be the time to store up for the storm. It may not be on the horizon or in the seven-day forecast, but at some point, there will be a storm, and you may only have the strength to rehearse what you know about God.

It's like when a snowstorm is projected all over the newscasts and people run out to get all the essentials for what I can only imagine is French toast—butter, eggs, milk, and bread. People are storing up for the storm. They are preparing for a time when they might not be able to leave their home because of the strength of the storm. We get that same chance to store up for our storms, for the moments when our faith is rocked or we go through something we never thought was supposed to be in the story. Now might be the time to go through the old journals and highlight the things that stand out to you, so that when your soul is zapped and tired, you can step into rehearsal and know that God was there then, and he is still here now.

He's fighting for you. On the days when the fog is thick and your hope is lost, place this truth around you like a life jacket: He's fighting for you. He's on your team. He's not giving up because you're precious to him—and, well, you're worth every fight.

I know that Fear is loud, and he wants to hiss into your mind that God is absent or that you are too weak to move forward. Don't worry about moving forward. Just stand still. He's fighting for you. You need only to stand still.

Chapter 16

Give Up the Ghosts

One Saturday night when I was a senior in college, I met a guy at a party. Without admitting it out loud, I was looking to fall in love. I was at a point where I felt "ready" to fall in love. I'd been independent throughout my four years of college, never really entertaining a date offer or pursuing a cute boy in my sociology classes, but I was getting to the point where I wanted someone to send texts back and forth to late into the night. I wanted someone to pick me up for dinner in his beat-up car and tell me I looked beautiful, even though the tanning beds made me look orange and I didn't know how to properly wax my eyebrows.

About an hour into the party, I noticed a guy standing in the doorway between the kitchen space and one of the dorm bedrooms. He was quiet and towered over the rest of the people at the party. I made my way over to talk to him. The conversation flowed easily. He was a biology major. He was Irish—very Irish. He talked about being one of seven siblings and I'll admit that my crazy girl brain watched him lean his head against the doorframe and imagined a big Irish thanksgiving.

At that moment, I felt chosen. Like his eyes were on me. I kept thinking to myself, *This is too simple and easy; there must be a catch.*

A few hours later, we left the party holding hands.

I remember walking out of the apartment and into a fog that

was thick in the air that night, as if the fog was sitting on a shelf that kept it at eye level. He walked me to the bus stop, where our paths would split. His dorm was down the hill, and my dorm was up the hill. There, at the bus station, he put his hand on the small of my back and leaned in for a kiss.

I wasn't expecting that, but before I could even react, he pulled away and just stared at me with a look of confusion in his eyes.

"Someone hurt you really badly in the past," he said to me after a silent moment. "I can see it in your eyes."

That's when I realized this guy needed to drop all of his biology classes and just find work as a scriptwriter for an angsty, young teen drama.

He took his hand off the small of my back and let his lanky arms fall to his sides.

"I don't want to be that guy to you, but if we keep this going, I will be."

With that, he kissed me on the forehead and walked away into the fog. He didn't ask for my number. He didn't say, "Let's chat soon." He just walked away into that fog.

I was thoroughly confused at this point, thinking this is the point where all my favorite characters from every popular TV drama are going to jump out from behind the bushes and scream, "GOT YA!"

I stood there for a little while longer before turning around to walk up the hill, straight into the fog. He was right though. More right than I wanted to admit. As much as I wanted to say I was ready to move forward and fall in love, I still had a ghost. That ghost had blue eyes.

For too long, I romanticized the idea that maybe one day, my ghost and I would meet up again in a coffee shop and things would be different—we'd be ready to try again. For so long I heralded that as the form of closure I needed to move on. I never realized a story that was never going to happen was holding me back. I had to release that story. I had to ask that ghost to leave.

When I got home to my apartment, I pulled out my laptop. I was finally, finally ready. Part of me was angry at the ghost, wanting to scream, "How long are you going to haunt me before I can have a normal relationship? Before I can be in love again? Why are you always coming up, and why am I forced to compare everyone else with you?"

What would I have told him if we were in the coffee shop? I knew, when I got honest with myself, that I wouldn't fight to keep him. But I would have forgiven him for how he hurt me. I would have told him I grew up and was doing okay and was on the cusp of all the things he wanted for me. I would tell him that for a very long time, I did things I thought would make him proud of me, but that was over after this night. I could no longer live to please a ghost. I had to step out into the world and do things because I wanted to make myself proud. Because it was enough to be proud of yourself, even if a blue-eyed boy could not applaud from the corner of the room.

I don't remember all the words of the letter I wrote to him, and I knew I would never send it, but I can tell you that it was enough for me to finally begin letting go and moving on with my life, no longer waiting for some kind of resolution to come or closure from a coffee shop. I had to give myself closure—an option that had been there all along.

And with that, I let him off the hook. I stopped blaming him for who he never became for me. I put the Word document in a folder called "Closure" and let go. Nothing in the room shifted. No earthquake took place when I signed my name and closed the laptop. There was no freaky Friday moment, but I did feel something in my chest. And I decided to call that thing closure.

Some people call it forgiveness. Other people call that feeling redemption. Sometimes it's just letting go, letting someone off the hook you placed them on. Either way, it was time to move forward.

I think sometimes we don't even realize we're being held back by things people did to us or the way things ended in the past. Things in life could look beautiful and everything could be rolling right along so we don't even realize there is more freedom to be experienced. The ghosts could go.

It may be a person holding you back. It may be a failed dream. It may be an idea of how life was "supposed" to look but never managed to meet your expectation. Whatever it is, we get to deal with the ghosts.

I call them ghosts because that's exactly what their demeanor is. They hang in the air. We can't always see them, but we feel them. And I think we get to call them out and tell them they cannot take up our space and time and relationships anymore. They cannot stamp a story of the past on our present and our future.

My dad tells a story about the time he chased the ghost of his grandfather out of his old home. The year was 1990. My cousin was only a few years old at the time, but he must have had enough words in his vocabulary to tell his mother he kept encountering a "strange man" in his room at night who would pace the room or sometimes sit quietly in the chair by the bed. It was my father who knew that his grandfather had died in that bedroom. He must have known this was the strange man visiting in the night. He decided to confront the ghost.

My father tells the story nonchalantly—like, one day he

walked into the bedroom of that old house and said, "Listen, you don't live here anymore. You need to stop coming around. You need to get out." That was it. One pep talk with the ghost of his grandfather, and my cousin's nighttime complaints ceased. I like the way my father tells the story because it just seems simple, like, "Yes, we get to call out the ghosts and take back control." It's as simple as that.

It may be that it's an honest conversation with yourself or someone else. Either way, I'd tell you to confront it so it cannot hold power over you any longer. It may be a lie you've embedded deep into your system, and the best course of action may be to get before God and become honest about it. Keep being honest. It might not leave in a day. It might not cease in a week. But if you keep hauling it into the light, I swear the thing that's holding you back will begin to lose power.

The thoughts that enter our brains become mind-sets if we hold on to them and accept them as truth. Before long, these mind-sets start to dictate what we think or do. They inform us of what we do or do not deserve. And they're quite convincing because the voice often sounds like our voice or that of someone we loved.

Mourning may be heavily involved in the process. You may have to mourn the person you didn't become. You may have to mourn the relationship that died. You may have to mourn the plans that didn't pan out. No one can tell you how long that mourning will last. No one can tell you when the pain will be gone, but you don't need to feel any shame in going through the motions of loss. A ghost is born out of loss. We're made more human by feeling the weight of that loss.

But at some point, on some beautiful day, you will know it's time to calmly tell the ghost, "I've mourned enough, and now

I'm saying goodbye to you. You cannot follow me into this next chapter. I must go on my own and walk into whatever is coming next." Because no matter what the size of that ghost is or the stories you've told yourself, you deserve to be free. You deserve to move forward unhindered by whatever was in your past.

Your story isn't over just because he didn't love you back. Your story isn't over because you made that mistake and now you think it should disqualify you. Your story isn't over because the expectation was popped or the ring didn't come or the baby didn't make it. You are allowed to pack up your things and leave the ghosts and ghost stories behind. That doesn't mean you will never mourn the loss again or feel the grief of things that didn't happen, but there is power in believing that these stories cannot hold you back, define you, or keep you from moving forward into new things.

Come on, come on, there are good and true and better stories up ahead.

Chapter 17

Step Out of the Woods

If you are going through the fire right now, I need you to block out all the noise and lean in close to read this: Keep on moving. Keep on moving forward, even if you feel faint. Now is not the time to put down your bags and unpack your luggage. Now is not the time to pitch a tent in the pit and decide to stay there for good. This is not the ending to your story, no matter what Fear tries to sing into you when you were all alone.

Draw in another breath of strength—I know you have it inside you. Isaiah 52:1 (ESV) reads, "Put on your strength." I think that's what you need to do. Like a well-loved denim jacket, put on any ounce of strength you have left. This season will not last forever. You are coming out of these woods.

Where you are standing right now might not be the most painful place you've ever been in. Things might be relatively okay, but what you feel sweeping over you like a thick fog is a fear of being unseen. I think we all go through these times when we feel largely anonymous. We feel like we're being kept away from the rest of the world and it's always going to be this way. But what if God is revealing the most he's ever revealed to you in the midst of this place, and you just haven't looked up yet? What if this isn't solitary confinement and instead it's training?

Every one of our stories has patches of the "unseen," whether we talk about them or not. Moses is known largely for parting seas and leading people out of captivity. But he had a beginning. And he had some false starts. At one point in the story, God plants his vision inside Moses. I'm sure you've felt it before. Suddenly you catch this bigger glimpse at what things "could be." It's the kind of vision that keeps you up at night. It leaves you breathless, thinking to yourself in the quiet of the middle of the night, *I might not be an accident.*

Moses jumps too soon though. He gets so passionate about his "one-day mission" that he careens out of control and starts that very second. The result? Some dude gets killed, and Moses has to go into hiding for forty years. Yikes!

I think about what Moses did during those forty years of hiding. He put down roots. He became a father. He tended a flock. If you think about leading an entire people group out of Egypt one day, applicable skills for dealing with unruly people would be (1) raising children and (2) herding dumb sheep.

It's easy to look at that story and think, *Well, I don't want to wait forty years for my destiny to unfold.* And that's not what I am prescribing for you. But I will say this: the seasons you want to discount may be more crucial than you realize.

What if Moses had neglected the flock because he was too busy thinking about the things he messed up or the people who were lapping him? The devil is in the business of keeping us distracted, keeping us convinced that we must watch the races of everyone around us to keep up, but we end up peddling on a stationary bike and going nowhere.

Even in the midst of this, when it feels like life has stalled for just you, God is still providing. Always providing. But we have to look up and pay close attention to see what's falling from the sky.

During a patch in my own story where I felt invisible, I called my friend Kelly, who always manages to set me straight.

"It just doesn't feel the same as it used to feel," I said to her. "I feel like I keep waiting for God to show up and take me out of this place, but nothing is shifting. God isn't providing."

"Is it that he's not providing?" she asked me. "Or is it just that he's not providing how you expect him to?"

Those two things are very different.

Kelly went on to tell me the story of a people group known as the Israelites, the ones God used Moses and Joshua to lead out of Egypt and into the Promised Land. And because God is a provider, he made manna fall from the sky for the Israelites. He provided for and nurtured them every day.

"But the story changed when they got to the edge of the land they were to go in to possess," Kelly said. "God stopped dropping the manna from heaven and gave the people a new method of provision, where they could grow crops and feed off the land."

"I think you may be waiting on the manna to fall again, but God isn't doing that anymore," Kelly said. "He's providing, but it looks different. You have to stop expecting to do the same old thing."

She was right. I was looking in the rearview mirror, waiting for God to show up in the ways he normally showed up for me. And it turns out that God wanted to do something different. Because that's just what he does. When you feel ready for more of the old, he comes up close and says, "Hey, I'm in the business of doing new things."

So that day, I sent the "take it away" prayer into retirement and picked a bigger prayer, one that takes more guts and grit to utter but for which the results are all around better: "God, help me move through this. You know I don't want to be here, and you know I would write a different story, but alas, I am here. So pull me in closer and help me learn as much as I can possibly learn for as long as we are here."

You may not see it right now, but I believe that one day you'll look back and remember how this season felt. You will remember the trees. You will remember the air. You will remember the days when God felt so present and the days when faith felt scarce. And because you took the notes and moved through it completely, you will be able to reach back your hand to help someone else walk through these same woods.

We don't usually think about suffering for the sake of other people, but I know, in my own life, that I'm beyond thankful for friends who, when life hit me hard, have shown up, nodded their heads, held my hand, and told me I wasn't crazy. They were only able to do this because they've walked the same route. They know how dark it can get. They know there will be openings in the trees eventually where the light pours through. They know what happens next.

I got an email the other day from a young woman named Chloe in which she told me how thankful she was that I had depression. It's an odd thing to thank someone for, but she said if I hadn't gone through the depression, she wasn't so sure she'd be able to walk out of hers. If you've ever hiked a trail before, you know what this means—you know that before you can follow the two red lines or the trail markers along the way, someone had to go before you and mark the trees. They had to find the way through and out. And because of that, you can confidently make steps in the right direction.

Our darkness may not be pretty, but it is purposeful. It turns us into brave fighters who know how to haul others out with the power of our testimonies. You only really know the true power of light when you place it in the darkness.

There will be purpose in your scars. You will live to tell these stories out loud. And someone, somewhere, whether we ever know it or not, might need you to keep enduring the pain and leaning into the fight, so they can know how to hold on longer when their own trials come.

Don't let the liars keep you up at night, trying to convince you that you're never coming out of this or that you have nothing to offer the world. Your scars mean something. This darkness means something. You are an anthem. You're a hymn and a song. You're a fighter, and you're a light. You're coming out of these woods.

You can keep praying the "take it away" prayer if you really want to. But if you want something different, you can try this one on for size: "Lord, place me where I'll grow the most. Teach me to love the dirt that transforms me. Give me eyes that see the golden threads in my pain. Let me be a lighthouse in this valley. Turn my story into a light that leads others out of the darkness."

Part 4

CHEERLEADERS

You're going to need people, and people are going to need you.

It's beautiful to realize that though we are all running toward different missions, we can still choose to make the glittery signs and be roadside cheerleaders for one another along the way.

Chapter 18

Make the Sign

I'm embarrassed to admit I lost so many precious hours in my twenties watching viral wedding proposals. It's a thing. For a while, it was a trend to plan out the most elaborate marriage proposals, record them as they were happening, and then post them on the internet for anyone to watch. You may be thinking, *Who has time to watch other people get engaged?* Me. I had time. I was a single girl who was starting to think she would be forever alone, and I don't know why I thought it would help my delicate psyche to watch other people experience one of the biggest moments of their lives while I cried all the mascara off my face and basically gave up hope that I would ever meet someone. Maybe I would meet someone, but it was unlikely they would send me up in a hot air balloon or orchestrate a flash mob with all of my friends and family popping out from behind trees and bushes.

If you don't believe that these kinds of proposals really exist, you need to go see for yourself. A simple Google search will do the trick. You will discover this trove of viral moments when the craftiest people in the world find some of the most impressive ways to get down on one knee and ask the other person, "Will you choose me? Will you spend the rest of your days choosing me?"

I think we live in a time when it's really easy to put our elaborate gestures on display for one another. It is even easier to catch yourself looking into the lens of other people's fireworks moments and wonder why your story doesn't look like their story. You start wanting that exact marriage proposal she got or that same ring. You start thinking life won't start until your pantry looks like hers or your wardrobe looks like his.

It's funny because we are all aware that social media is, and has been, a highlight reel for a long time. So many of us would be quick to say, "It isn't real" and "That story doesn't tell the whole story," but in small ways, we still believe the stories. We still think our lives would be better if _____ would happen.

But maybe that's not where our eyes need to be fixed. Maybe that doesn't matter as much as we think it does.

When I think back to my wedding—one of those fireworks moments that is supposed to stand out in your life—I don't remember the big event. I remember the smallest things. The tiniest details. The little gestures. I remember the playlist one of my girlfriends put together for us as we were getting ready. I remember Lane and me staying up late the night before the wedding to write cards to each guest attending because we wanted them to feel chosen and seen. I remember a little red cooler showing up at the door a few weeks before the wedding, a gift from one of my friends who was too sick at the time to travel to Atlanta for the occasion, and how that little red cooler meant everything to me.

I remember the fake snow that my wedding planner had the genius idea of ordering. I still don't know how he located bio-degradable snow, but he filled buckets with it, and all the guests got a chance to pick up a pile of "snow" with their bare hands as we were leaving the wedding so they could chuck it at us. I just remember how happy everyone was about the snow, how cool it was to see Southerners who rarely got a snowflake, never mind a snowstorm, throwing fake snow in the air three weeks before Christmas.

I remember one point in the evening when the dance floor was so rowdy and alive that all the guys held Lane in the air as he crowd-surfed across the dance floor. I remember standing back to see my brother and some cousins I don't see very often, mixed in with Lane's best friends and my best friends, all holding Lane up, laughing and singing to the music. I took several mental notes of that moment because that was my favorite part of the evening.

It wasn't the bigness of the event or the elaborate parts of the evening that I will carry in my memory—it's the small stuff. It's the way he looked at me. How he opened the door for me when we got into the car to drive off to the hotel. How I wore sneakers under my dress and how the heels never made an appearance. How my dad looked as he waited to walk me down the aisle.

We think it's about the bigness, but it rarely is. We think it's about how we can make the next big reveal or prove to other people that our lives are on fire, but a life well lived is just a collection of small gestures and people you love the best you can and stories we tell back to one another when the moment has passed.

We grow up thinking adulthood is going to be all these big, impressive things and it turns out to be the small things and the people that stand out to us, that make us feel like we are right here and there is nothing we would change. At the end of our lives, I don't think we will compare to-do lists or stack our accomplished goals in a pile to show off. We won't even really remember those elaborate gestures so much as we will remember people—what they said to us, how they made us feel, how God used us to stitch fight songs back into the hearts of others when all hope seemed lost.

The best thing I can tell you is this: pay attention to the nudges.

There will be nudges. When you start being open to how God wants to use you as a participant in the story, you may get these crazy sorts of nudges to do something or say something, and you may immediately shut down and say, "That wasn't God. I'm just going crazy and I'm hearing voices."

It's sweet to hear from God when the words are kind and directed at you. It's harder to say, "I am listening and willing to do anything" when the nudge from God looks like reaching out to a person or showing up on their doorstep.

I was talking to a young woman named Kate recently who had been trying to make her prayers bolder than ever before. She felt disconnected from God and stuck in her own pain, but she knew she wanted to crawl out. She was going through a hard time financially, raising five kids, and feeling alone and isolated.

She prayed that God would start to use her to help others, to help her be a tool. And God did it. And then she freaked out and tried to retreat and take back prayers from the heavens without God noticing. But the nudge he gave her kept getting stronger, and she had to remind herself that when she said, "Anything, God," she meant any awkward, weird, unsettling, out of character thing.

The nudge told Kate to make cookies and bring them to her neighbor down the street. She didn't want to. She knew that the woman down the street had recently lost a young child. It was weighty and heavy—and how could cookies help anyway?

"I don't want to take them to her," she said to God. She didn't feel comfortable enough to step into that grief.

But she made the cookies. And I'm betting she worried and doubted the whole time she cracked the eggs and mixed the dough. And then she marched down the street (or she probably begrudgingly dragged her feet) and knocked on the woman's door. Her husband answered and went to get his wife. Kate said she stood there for nearly ten minutes waiting, wrestling with God the entire time.

When the woman arrived at the door, she looked tired and disheveled, as if she'd been crying for weeks. She stared at Kate with the plate of cookies in her hands, and then she finally spoke.

"Did you know that today is the four-week anniversary of my son's death?" She stopped. "I've been asking God for help today. I haven't been able to get out of bed."

Kate said something came over her at that moment. She grabbed the woman and pulled her in. She said to her, "God told me to come."

As the woman cried in Kate's arms, she said back, "I know. I know he did."

This is what I mean about those nudges. They happen all the time and it's important that we don't miss them. The thing is, we get really good at (1) being distracted, (2) explaining them away, or (3) just flat out saying no. When it doesn't seem like God is doing something elaborate with us, it's tempting to assume that the ordinary acts don't matter.

You and I will miss those crucial nudges if we get so internally focused on the "me, me, me" anthems in our brains. If we get so focused on what we need that we forget that our friends need encouragement. My mom needs encouragement. My husband needs encouragement. And these people don't just need encouragement in the form of a text sent once or twice a week. They need real movements of love. They need people who show up fully to the task of cheering them on with home-cooked meals and a willingness to painstakingly read IKEA instructions or babysit for them at the last minute. They don't need a phantom who provides encouragement and then ghosts. They need people who step fully into the race with them.

I can tell you from experience that stepping into someone else's race to push them forward is one of the more fulfilling tasks you will ever take part in. You may not think that at first, and you may not always feel like showing up, but I can promise you that something will start to shift in your heart as you become a cheerleader for other people. Something will change, and no amount of good sentences or words will be able to truly capture what that feeling is. I have to believe that God knit and designed a special feeling that is only unlocked when we put people in front of ourselves and push them to be bright.

There are going to be the nudges that make you feel crazy, but what if you listened to them anyway? What if you went out on a limb and just decided to follow through? What would change? Who might God bless through you?

I often think that when a person pops up randomly in my mind for the first time in a long time, I should take that as a nudge, as a reason to reach out and say, "Hey, I thought of you today, and here are a few things I'm praying about today." I send the texts because I've never been upset or let down or perturbed to get that kind of text from someone else.

If we break the nudges down into simple tasks that become the overarching themes of our stories rather than footnotes, I think God can unleash all sorts of crazy hope into the world through us.

I have a friend named Christina who walked with me during a time when I lost a close friend. It was one of the more painful things I've ever experienced, and even when the dust had settled, it left me triggered by the fear that I wasn't a good friend.

Christina swooped in, noticed the fear, and continually chose moments to say to me, "You are a good friend." We could be having a conversation that had nothing to do with friendship, and she would simply say, "You are a good friend." She does this all the time, even now that we're years removed from the incident. She knows the fears that jangle around inside me, and she makes the effort to combat them with the truth.

This is all of us. Every single one of us has fears and worries and doubts. The people you love—they are walking around this earth today with all sorts of worries, doubts, and fears rattling around inside of them. Some of them you know, and some of them you can't even imagine. But you and I don't need to know everything about everyone in order to pick up the phone and call, just because, or take five minutes to craft a text of encouragement.

But "seeing people" and then becoming active in encouraging them aren't accidental things. We have to clear the space for it. It means saying no to other things that honestly give me no life in order to make space to be a light to others. It means not tuning out when a sermon doesn't strike me or hit me where I'm at and realizing that maybe I'm meant to listen so I can pass these words to someone else. It means saying yes to the interruptions and the ways people hijack our days on a continual basis with their laughter, their needs, their gestures, and their presence.

I want to be that kind of person. I want to take the time to know the fears of my friends. I want to remember to say, "Happy birthday." I want to slow down and bake the cookies and really have time to look people in the eye and speak to their fears. I want to not be so frantic with the running and jumping to get all the things on the list checked off, because my people matter more than tasks to accomplish.

At any point in the story, you can become the kind of person who clears enough space to grab the poster board and make the glittery sign for someone who needs it as they run their race. You can show up in the cold and the rain and the heat to walk and run those metaphorical miles alongside someone. You can stand in the front row of their story, pump your fist in the air, and remind them of this: we don't give up; we just keep getting better.

What if we believed in the "long distance" of one another like that? What if we stopped treating this life as a solo race and started seeing the deeper threads of a relay? Of a passing of the baton? Of spurring one another on and picking up the slack when someone else is tired. It would be more beautiful, that's for sure.

It won't always be easy, and the moments you have with other people won't always turn out how you envisioned them in your mind. But if you can stay present in the story you're living out with others, you won't miss a thing.

I promise you—you won't miss a thing.

Chapter 19

Hold Me in the Light

"I will hold you in the light."

That's what the Quakers say when they want someone to know they'll be praying constantly for them: "I will hold you in the light."

It's a powerful image to think about, the idea that there are going to be times when the dark feels endless and our faith is frail and on the verge of hospice. Times when we can't find the words to mumble or pray. Those will be the times in my story and yours when we will need someone to stretch out their arms and hold us in the light for as long as it takes to return to walk out of the dark woods.

Several years ago, I had the opportunity to work with a national flower company for a Valentine's Day campaign. We created a love letter writing hotline. Instead of taking complaints and doing basic customer service, the company formed an entirely new call center station, where twenty outstanding employees would be transformed into love letter writing coaches. For the whole month of February, anyone could call into the hotline and say, "Help. I need help writing the note to go with the flowers I'm sending," and these experts would coach them through the process.

As part of the job, I went on a radio tour. It was a two-day span in which I went on nearly forty radio stations to talk about the love letter hotline.

As we were setting up the tour, I was told I needed to use a landline phone. I didn't have a landline phone for the radio tour, so the company booked me a hotel room about forty minutes north of the city, and I waited by the hotel phone for the next two days.

In my mind, this sounded luxurious—like a mini vacation. Just me in a hotel room taking calls and relaxing. In the mind of Lane, the man I'd been dating for the last five months at this time, it sounded like a disaster because, as much as I say I like to be alone, I get very depressed in a short span of solitude. I'm not someone who does well spending two days alone in a hotel room with no breaks to leave.

At around 9:00 p.m. on that first day in the hotel room, I was fried. I'd taken about thirty calls by that time, and I was feeling all the feelings Lane had predicted—depression, anxiety, loneliness.

Without even being asked, Lane showed up that evening to bring me dinner and check in on me.

When I got down to the hotel entrance to let him in, he could see the look of fatigue and defeat on my face.

"I'm coming upstairs with you," he said to me. I nodded and led him up to the room.

When we got to the room, he took my hands and said to me, "We are going over to the bed, and we're going to lie down, okay? I'm going to hold you until all the depression is out of you, okay?"

I complied, not having the energy to do much more, and that's what happened for the next hour or so. He held me tight, and I cried buckets, and we prayed to God that the depression would just leave. As I cried out, I thought about how different my life had looked a year before when I was fighting for my life through a constant fog of daily depression, how I could have only dreamed of someone to physically hold me through that storm the way Lane knew how to hold me now.

Sometimes we show up to do the holding. Sometimes we show up to make the tea. Sometimes we show up, and someone we love is in the most unimaginable circumstances, and no matter how much we want to rescue them, all we can do is sit with them and find ways to hold them in the light until the darkness starts to fade.

We should never discount these events in the story line. They matter. Sometimes showing up to be the quiet cheerleader is the most important work you will ever do.

Jesus was big on this. He brought it up quite frequently that we could help people and pray for people without needing to make a big stink about it. He said it wasn't about the show or the applause; it was simply about serving people because we have his hands and we have his feet and we sometimes are the only introduction that people ever get to him. But he said a lot about getting away with God to pray, about closing the door and praying in secret so no one could see you.

I think this is one of the most important things we can do for others who are lost or tired or losing hope—to get in the closet, close the door, and pray for them. To listen for what God has to say and to be the messenger of hope when necessary.

People often ask me if I would go through the depression of 2014 again if I had a choice or say in the matter. My answer is yes. One thousand times yes. Because in the thick of the fog I learned how to listen to God in the dark.

During that time, I kept expecting God to show up in my prayer time and say something like, "Do this, this, and this, and you will be healed," or at least give me a timeline of when the illness would be ending so I could mark something on the calendar. But there was a lot of silence and doubt. People texted prayers and things they heard from God continually throughout that time. I held on to those messages. They were life jackets showing up to keep me afloat.

Even though there was a long period where I didn't hear God, I still showed up day after day and cried out to him. I'd sit there and just wait to hear something, anything that would give me a glimpse of hope.

On the bedroom floor one morning, I waited on God. I waited to hear him speak and give me any kind of breadcrumb to hold on to. It was there, in that listening, that I heard my own three words: Pray for Laney.

Pray for Laney. That was it. I scribbled it down, and I started right there on the spot to pray for Laney. I didn't know how Laney was, but I imagined her somewhere, maybe in her own dark space, struggling to get out of bed or to believe that any of this matters. I started praying for her daily, waiting for her to show up. I imagined I'd pray for a few days and then get an email from a girl named Laney, who would go on to tell me all these things in her life that needed prayer and fixing. Day after day, I checked my email, but Laney wasn't there.

Days went by, and Laney never showed up. Months went by, and Laney never showed up. I still thought about her and had some moments when I thought that maybe I heard it wrong. Regardless, there had to be a Laney out there somewhere, and wherever they were, even if they never knew it, they were being covered in thick and weighty prayers.

Nine months later, I was walking out of recovery and getting better every day. I had new strength and a new appreciation for life. I was surrounded by good people, and I was dating someone new, someone who made me feel like I had been a prayer of their own for a very long time.

We went on dates. We texted until late in the evenings. We woke one another up with phone calls. And then we made it official by becoming Facebook friends. And as I scrolled through his page for the very first time (because now would be the time to check for crazy red flags, and social media is where you often find them), I came across a post from his mother. It contained a picture of her and him standing outside the loft where I'd just been days before, eating a home-cooked meal and making brownies alongside him.

The post was from August of that year, though it was October now.

"Laney's first home," the post read. *Laney.*

I immediately texted him and asked, Wait, do you go by the name Laney?

"Yeah," he responded. "I mean, just with my family and closest friends. But that is what they've been calling me for years. Laney. Laney Belle."

I don't know how it hadn't clicked before, how I hadn't put the pieces together, but it was in that moment that I knew without a doubt: Laney is here. Laney showed up. Laney is real after all.

I had no clue that I was praying for a man who, at the time my prayers were being uttered, was going through his own period of darkness and doubt—a season when everything felt weighty, and he felt like, "God, is she ever coming?" It would be that season that would build in him the strength to pack up his things and move to the city of Atlanta. As it turns out, in the darkest time of my life, God handed me a glimmer of what was to come, and I didn't know it yet, but I am so thankful I had the chance to hold that boy in the light before he ever had a chance to hold me.

And when the time was right—and not a day sooner—that boy showed up at my door in a white O.J. Bronco to pick me up for our first date.

I didn't know Laney would be the man who'd take care of me when I was sick. I didn't know Laney would be the guy who would build all the furniture in my office or propose to me in a backyard strung with twinkle lights in July in front of all the people I loved most dearly. I didn't know Laney would be waiting at the end of the aisle—that when I thought the story might be over soon, God was just making room for the second act. And the second act has been so much better than the first.

Two years into our marriage, we began the conversation about having kids one day. It was just the initial conversation, the one where you google meanings of names and give names to kids who don't exist yet. I told him how much I thought about a child whose name simply meant "light" because that's my favorite word in the English language. It is because of the light piercing through the darkness that I am still here today. It is a reminder of prayers said over and over again that the light would just pour through.

We started this conversation while Lane was driving me to the airport, so in the middle of it, he dropped me off and kissed me goodbye. As I rolled my bag into TSA Precheck, I pulled out my phone and googled "names that mean light" just to see what was there. There, in the center of the list, sat the words:

LANEY—RAY OF LIGHT

On any given day, your friends and people you know are saying prayers. I don't know where it all happens, but I know dialogues with God are ensuing all over the place. They are happening in cars. They are happening on trains. They are happening in quiet rooms and loud stadiums. All over the place, your friends are going places, touching the world, and saying prayers. We are all praying some sort of prayer. Some are crying out to God, and some don't know who they're crying out to yet. If we don't stop to listen, how will we ever know if we held one of their answers? How would we know if we were the ones who could hold them in the light when they needed it the most?

Sometimes you pray, and sometimes you are the answered prayer.

I think this requires that we don't treat God like a cashier at Target who processes our transactions, hands us our bags, and moves on to the next person. We have to get good at the waiting and listening part; we have to learn how to be in his presence without expecting a thing.

"I will hold you in the light."

You can always begin with those seven words if you don't know where to start or if you're fumbling over your words. It's a simple way to tell someone, "I see you. I'm right with you. I'm holding you in the light, and I will not move from this posture. Your faith may feel restless, and it may all seem dark right now, but I'm standing beside you and believing that your story will turn the corner. Just hold on a little longer. The light is coming. It's going to pour through."

Chapter 20

Walk Me through the Rain

The first day I met Bebe, I knew he was a walking, talking answer to a prayer I'd been repeating under my breath for the last month or so. As Lane and I went through the motions—and theatrics—of buying a house, I kept praying that we would move into a place where we would have neighbors. Real neighbors. In the place we lived for the first two years of marriage, people couldn't even be bothered to say hello or ask how you were doing. It was a strange environment, made stranger by the fact that we were literally a wall away from some people, and we never had conversations or ever brought them soup when they got sick.

I want this though. I want the feel of a neighborhood, where people come to your door and sit on your porch and talk to you. I haven't lived in the Bronx for ten years, but I still cannot duplicate what I found there anywhere else. I still wake up missing the people who wanted to bring food and clothes and all sorts of flowers and gifts just because you were their neighbor. I hope I never forget how it felt.

The day we opened the door to our house, Bebe was there to greet us. It was the week before Christmas, and he came up to us on a bicycle. He wore a blue ski hat with the word SECURITY on it in crooked letters. One of the first things he asked was,

"Can you cook?" I nodded yes. "Can you make me a Christmas dinner?" I nodded yes.

It was five days before Christmas, and I'm not the best cook. But I am getting better with each passing meal. I was beyond thrilled to try out my cooking skills with Bebe and may have gone a little overboard with his Christmas dinner. His feast featured honey mustard chicken, green beans, and sweet potatoes—big pots of food that would last for days. This was the start of our friendship.

In the days that followed, Bebe would wedge his way into our hearts. He came to the door at least once a day to check on us. He rode his bicycle around the streets at all hours, as he proudly told us, more than a couple times, "I'm security for this neighborhood. I got a shift over on the next street."

We've never gotten the full story from Bebe, but we know some of the facts (I think). Bebe technically lives in the house across the street from us, but he doesn't own it and doesn't pay rent. He established a relationship with the owner of the home, a guy who'd bought several homes on the block to flip and resell. It must be a trust-filled relationship because the man lets Bebe stay in the house throughout the process of being flipped. He doesn't have running water, so he uses ours. He is a new man come springtime because his lawn business can thrive again. Come spring, you'll find Bebe hauling his lawnmower up and down the streets. He's a self-proclaimed "BOSS," and you can ask anyone on the street about Bebe. Everyone knows him. Everyone loves him. Everyone respects him.

When we have people over, Bebe operates as "security" for us as he calls it. He approaches every person who parks on the street and asks them, "Are you here to see my family?" We threw a surprise party for Lane's parents and asked Bebe to be our security.

He was flawless that night, guiding traffic and greeting people. We invited him to the party later that evening, and I'll never forget the way his eyes glowed as he came in from the cold for a few minutes to make a heaping plate of tacos and nachos. He went around the party and introduced himself to every person with a handshake. "This is my family," he kept telling our family. "God put them here for me."

I feel the same way, Bebe. God put you here for me.

Since our neighborhood is considered a developing one, there is still some crime that happens. This is just part of living in a city. A few months into living there, we woke up to loud banging, and we were almost certain someone was slamming on our door. Lane got to up to check the house, but there was no evidence that anyone had been there at all. It was just past midnight. We cuddled close and went back to sleep.

In the morning, I approached Bebe and asked if he had seen anyone banging on our door during the night.

"Oh, girl," he sighed and said to me. "That wasn't no banging . . . those were gunshots."

I knew something like that was bound to happen eventually, but it still shakes you good to hear gunshots so close to you for the first time. But later that day, there was a knock on the door. It was Bebe, clad in his winter coat that used to be Lane's. He reached out his hand to give me something—a petite pink bottle of pepper spray. It was his way of saying, "I'll do what I can to protect you."

Bebe and I have a special relationship because we both treat one another like an answer to prayer. I cook his meals or make extra coffee for him while giving him dating advice. He rings the doorbell in the morning just to check on me when Lane leaves, and then he always waves me off by saying, "Remember, don't work too hard. You work hard enough." We get one another. And he's also a confidence booster because there hasn't been a single day when Bebe doesn't say, "You look beautiful" or "You look strong" or "You look like a boss." I'm convinced that the world needs more Bebes in it. My favorite is the way he says goodbye to everyone he meets: "If no one thought to tell ya today, I love you."

One evening, it was pouring as I drove home from a friend's house. I pulled into the driveway, turned off the car, and sat there for a few minutes, waiting for the rain to subside. It's only a few yards between the driveway and the porch, but I was dreading the sprint.

Tap. Tap. Tap.

I looked to my left to see Bebe standing outside the window of the car. He had seen me pull up, so he walked across the street with an umbrella hoisted in the air. He had come out of his house just to walk me to my door. Just to walk me through the rain so I wouldn't get drenched. Together we walked down the driveway and across the yard until I got onto the front porch.

I thanked him and told him he didn't have to go out of his way like that to walk me inside.

"This is what neighbors are for," Bebe said as he turned to walk back to his house. "If no one thought to tell ya today, I love you." He closed the umbrella as soon as he got across the street and walked inside.

This is what neighbors are for. His words stirred in me as I unloaded my bag and stripped off the layers of winter clothes. This is what it is all for. This is what makes it all worthwhile, that we tap on each other's windows on the day we've got an umbrella handy and walk one another through the rain. That we spot the people who need help. That we are their best cheerleaders and allies, never taking a second more to ask whether or not they're worthy to be loved. Bebe teaches me the gospel daily as he shows up, selflessly, to be the example of what a real neighbor looks like.

If ever I start to doubt why I'm here or what I need to do with this day to make it count, I can circle back to that memory of Bebe walking me just a few yards through the rain—and I suddenly know. I don't doubt anymore why I am here and what I was made to do. I'll be a better neighbor. I'll be a better cheer-leader. I'll be the one with the umbrella hoisted in the air, ready to help others walk on through as we find shelter from the rain.

Part 5

STEADY PACES + FINISH LINES

When you keep fighting and keep committing, things start to change.

You find a steady pace, and you encounter what it takes to show up for the long haul.

Chapter 21

Look How Far We've Come

I've been an armchair detective of sorts since I was nine years old. After the JonBenét Ramsey case showed up all over the news, I became obsessed with solving the case. I read every book. I took notes on every website I could find. I made folders for evidences, folders for photos, and folders for suspects. I was ten years old and believed I found my purpose in life. I think I liked the prospect of unsolved cases so much because my grandmother is a crime junkie as well. She'd always ask me if there was any news or new evidence I'd discovered in the case, and I was proud to spread out my latest research and show her what I'd found. These are my best memories with my grandmother—she and I showing up to crack the cases at the dining room table. She stoked this fire in me, and I'm thankful for that.

But I've read enough books and watched enough documentaries to know that most cases that go on to be solved end up in a courtroom for a trial. Two sides will present their cases and, more importantly, their evidence. Cases hinge on evidence (or at least the just ones hang on evidence) because evidence translates into proof. So if you show up to a courtroom with no evidence at all, it is much harder to win the case.

Fear wants to take you into the courtroom on a daily basis, and so it hungers for evidence it can use against you.

When you are making progress, Fear will find some loophole to talk down to you or convince you to stand still. Fear has a handful of remarks that he thinks are so original: You're not doing enough. You wasted the day. Other people are doing so much more than you are.

I used to confuse the voice of Fear with the voice of God. For a long time, I thought God was waiting for me to increase my productivity. I was talking to my mom on the phone one day, and I told her, "I feel guilty when I sleep in. I feel like God would say to me, 'Girl, where were you this morning? I could have used you. Because you weren't up, I had to go use someone else.'"

My mom laughed and responded, "Oh no, that's not how God sounds. God would totally say, 'Sleep, girl. I'll use you when you wake up.'"

I've had to get crafty to deal with my fear. So what do I do now that I didn't do before? I collect evidence.

All the time, I collect evidence of who I am becoming and how God is growing me and how far I've come.

Now maybe this sounds exhausting to you, but I'm not saying I count every step and put every movement of my life into a spreadsheet, but I have developed the discipline of tracking progress because otherwise my anxious brain will convince me that no progress was made. That's the stupid truth about anxiety—it doesn't have a reliable leg to stand on, and yet we still listen to it.

At some point, Fear is going to try to convince you that you are making no progress, and I can speak from experience that he has a pretty convincing case. When you collect evidence, you have something to throw back in Fear's face.

Because I track my words, I'm able to say to Fear, "It's sweet that you want to make a claim that my words don't matter, but I have evidence of more than two hundred thousand words I wrote this year. And sorry, Fear, but there is no way that God won't use that abundant supply to encourage others."

So then Fear will tell me I'm making no real progress in my health journey because the numbers on the scale aren't moving. Because I track my workouts, I can come back and say politely to Fear, "Well, that's silly. I've done dozens of workouts in the last few months that have made me stronger and more confident, and they've pushed me into new zones of endurance I didn't think were possible. So no, I don't measure by the scale; I measure by strength."

I always say discipline is like a muscle—you need to show up consistently to see results. And as you get stronger and the habits start to stack up, you can show up to help someone else flex their own discipline muscles.

Last year, Lane and I bought our first house together. The first time we walked into the house to see it, we prayed a prayer that if God would give us this house, we would keep the doors open for anyone who arrived. The prayer was answered, and the doors have stayed open ever since.

But it's crazy to think it would be that seamless. And you're right, it wasn't that seamless. Two weeks after moving into our new home, I remember Lane coming home one morning from work at 10:00 a.m.

I'll never forget how defeated and sad he looked as he stood in the doorway and said, "They let me go. I don't have a job anymore." He walked into the bedroom to take off his work-clothes, and the two of us didn't know how to process the news other than being shocked into silence.

We were three weeks into living in a new house and dealing

with a new mortgage. We hadn't sold our old apartment yet. We were due to start paying two mortgages at the end of February if a buyer didn't materialize. It took everything in us not to say to God, "This isn't how we thought the start of a new year would look. How are we going to handle this?"

But can I tell you that a supernatural strength that never existed in me before rose up that day. Lane is always optimistic and bright when I am having a freak-out moment, and so I needed to be strong and hold it together for him.

We decided a few unspoken things that day:

1. We would choose praise in advance. No matter the circumstance, we were going to keep thanking God for the eventual outcome.

2. We would see this as an opportunity for better. It would have been easy at that moment to turn toward the rearview mirror and ask, "What could we have done differently?" But there was no point in that. It would only fuel more fear. We were going to say yes to the circumstances and trust they would make us better in the end.

3. We would fight this out with our closest people. Meaning, we only told a few people what happened. We told people we knew would pray instead of talk. We could have made a big announcement and cast our nets wide for job opportunities, but we trusted that God wanted us to walk this out without freaking out—and you really can start freaking out pretty easily when the list of people who know starts to grow longer and longer.

The following day, Lane and I sat down to draw a map for his days. He was going from ten hours of work a day to no work at all, so we gave him some structure. Time to do job applications. Time for reading his Bible. Time to get some exercise in. We even built in time for him to read during the day, a hobby he'd wanted to pick up but just couldn't make the habit stick since we'd started dating.

And what happened in those next three and a half months is only something God can take the credit for. A buyer for the apartment showed up the week Lane lost his job and asked that the process be expedited. They wanted to close on February 28—exactly one day before we were due to start paying for two mortgages. With the close of the sale, Lane had just enough money to kill the credit card debt he'd been working aggressively to pay off for the last year. I experienced a flurry of extra work that was much needed in our time as a single-income family.

Best of all, I watched Lane flourish under new discipline. I watched him become more confident, but in a quiet way. I watched him create patterns, rhythms, and routines that were balanced. I watched him take a time when he might be tempted to feel like a failure or struggle for hope and use the space as an opportunity to better himself.

Months after this point, Lane has a new job, but he is still showing up to the daily disciplines he established during a period that could have otherwise been seen as a dark spot in our story. Daily, we collect evidence that proves, without a doubt, how we are growing. We are growing in health. We are growing in our communication with God. We are growing in our marriage. We are growing in our habits and hobbies.

It doesn't mean every day is easy, but I can confidently say that nothing we do is hinged on motivation. There are just some days when the motivation won't be there, when we cannot be our own best cheerleader, and that's where it matters that discipline has taken root inside us and latched on for the long haul.

Here's the best part about collecting evidence of how you've grown: you get the chance to look back and see just how far you've come.

I am on a prison ministry team at my church, where we go into a correctional institution here in Atlanta to serve. At this institution, the women have fewer than five years in their sentence. Some of them wear uniforms, while others are able to leave the premises, go to work, and wear street clothes as they get closer to reentering society.

Once a month, a team of us shows up to put on an event for the women living there. We dress the tables with beautiful tablecloths and flowers. We make table settings. We cater in some of the best food in Atlanta, and each of us is assigned to a table for the evening.

We serve salad and main courses, coffee and dessert. Then when we are full to the brim, we stand to our feet and worship together. We pray together. We share our stories with one another.

One evening, I sat next to three women who had just arrived at the transitional center that morning. They told me they'd been awakened at 2:30 a.m. and shuffled into buses to get here. The ride took about three hours. Their day had been filled with new procedures, new rules, and new people. None of them thought the long day would end with sitting at a fancy table being served barbecue and apple pie.

As the evening wound down, I led a discussion at my table based on the message we had listened to. One of the questions was, "What does success look like to you?"

I thought this might be a silly or a naive question to ask. I worried about what the responses could be coming from this space in their lives. But one woman spoke up immediately—one of the three who had arrived that day.

"Well," she said, "I kind of think this is success." She made a gesture as if she was taking in the whole room and the atmosphere. "We just got here today, and this party is happening. It feels like a homecoming party—like God is showing us how far we've come in all of this."

The women around the table nodded, and I nodded too, tears in my eyes. *Yes*, I thought to myself. *This is evidence. This is collected evidence that each of us has come so far. That we are not the people we used to be. That even if we wished we could undo some things from the past, there was no point in not looking at how this day stands out as progress. We are living proof of a better song.*

So we celebrate. We cheer. We thank God for the progress, even when it may feel small. And with more baby steps and little wins, we can travel down the road toward better. And then one day farther down the line, I want to believe we will look back down the long road we traveled and be able to say, "Wow, I've made it farther than I ever imagined. Look how far we've come. This is success to me. This is definitely success to me."

I would never suggest that you become neurotic about counting everything in your life as evidence of moving forward, but I think we need to get better at celebrating the little wins. We can only do this if we know when the wins arrive. How are we supposed to look back and say, "Look how far I've come," if we haven't even drawn a map to prove we've been taking steps?

Journals are maps. Bibles with notes scribbled in the margins are maps. Planners are maps. Prayer journals are maps. These maps take discipline to create, but they are evidence that God has moved, that we have followed, that growth has come. These things matter because they are evidence against Fear's case that we have not grown in the last few years.

Because, trust me, there will come a day when Fear punches you good, and you may forget for a second or two who you really are. I wish I could sit with you on those days, take your hands, and say boldly to you, "When you feel you're not yourself or when you think you can't move forward, collect evidence of the opposite." Fear will want to feed you all sorts of lies, but you can combat those weak, desperate anthems by collecting evidence of the opposite.

Collecting evidence doesn't mean you will always rule the day or make all the things happen. Some days I feel plain pathetic, and on those days, I pull out a stack of sticky notes and write down every little task I make happen. I line my computer and desk with the sticky notes, so that even if I don't feel like myself, there's evidence all around me that I've taken steps forward.

Collecting evidence, slowly but consistently, means you can no longer accept the lie that you've not moved and become someone different. You are becoming someone different with every prayer you pray, every workout you commit to, every time you step into the Word of God, every vitamin you take, every person you show up for. This collection of evidence is proof that you lived and that you pursued discipline—and because of that consistency, you experienced freedom and incredible growth.

Don't believe the lies that Fear wants to feed you about being behind or never moving forward. Look at all the evidence that supports the opposite of that claim. Just look at how far you've come.

Chapter 22

Step Back in Love

I started an accidental global movement when I was twenty-two years old. I was fresh out of college and surprised to find that I had missed the course in college where they tell you what to do after you graduate. If I could, I would go back to college and create that course for others. In the curriculum, we'd cover all the strange feelings that come from leaving college. How to let go. How to not live in the past. How to be okay when the dream job doesn't arrive. How to live, and live well, that first year out.

Because I didn't know how to cope with the feelings of sadness and disillusionment that rose up all around me, I ended up leaving love letters across New York City for strangers to find. It sounds very poetic, but I was just a really sad girl trying to find her way and maybe encourage someone else in the process.

What I didn't anticipate is that I would end up building an organization so others could do the same thing. After blogging about those first letters that I left around New York City, it was evident there was no turning back. People wanted to know about the love letters. People only cared about the love letters. People wanted to join in.

So I built the organization, and I prayed to God that I would be able to love this thing well in the process. And he answered that prayer. For a long time, I was on fire. I would give anything to be able to hand you those feelings at some point in your life—the feelings that make you say, "There's no time to sleep because the present moment is just too good."

If you're lucky, you will encounter these feelings in your lifetime, and there will be no real way to catch them in a jar or make them last. They will come in spurts and they will make everything else around you seem electrifying. The best thing I can tell you is to cherish them while they last.

I tell anyone who is just starting out with some dream that seems exhilarating and promising to soak up those beginner feelings. Soak up the moments that make you feel like you're unstoppable, like you're creating something beautiful in the extra hours of the day. Soak up the late nights and extra cups of coffee that keep you burning the midnight oil. Soak up the tired eyes and the wired feeling that come from tapping into untapped potential. This is what's all there when you're creating something new, and it feels like it's just you and God taking on the rest of the world. Those feelings are beautiful, and they should be savored. But you shouldn't be dismayed when they don't last forever.

Those feelings stopped for me. They died out—somewhere around the two- or three-year mark. The tasks became mundane. The emails began to feel repetitive. I started to secretly despise when someone would call me the "love letter girl" or "the love letter lady." God was using this story to touch the hearts of many, but I was beginning to wish that he wouldn't. I was letting my feelings overtake the chance to grow and change. I'd made a grave mistake—I made the whole thing all about me and stopped seeing those who needed it just as much as I'd needed it at the age of twenty-two, when I was lost and trying to find my way.

When I thought I was falling out of love, I thought that was it. I thought because of my feelings that it must be time to close up shop and give up. I saw the wilting and didn't choose to lean in and cultivate; I chose to lean out and avoid the feelings.

That's the dangerous part.

The feeling of "falling out of love" isn't a dangerous thing so much as it is a feeling to face. The dangerous part was choosing to give in to the feeling and grow stagnant because of the feeling. The danger came when I chose resentment over gratitude. When I chose resignation over reinvention.

Like I said before, you'll fall out of love. The feelings will fade. The honeymoon period will slip into the background, and you'll ask yourself defining questions you never thought you'd ask, like, "Was I ever in love to begin with? Why can't I just go back to that place?"

I know now it wasn't really that I was falling out of love; it was that God was taking me through a process of staying in love. And the process of staying in love with something or someone is often a painful one. Oswald Chambers writes:

Ever since God gave us the vision, He has been at work. He is getting us into the shape of the goal He has for us, and yet over and over again we try to escape from the Sculptor's hand in an effort to batter ourselves into the shape of our own goal.

The vision that God gives is not some unattainable castle in the sky, but a vision of what God wants you to be down here. Allow the Potter to put you on His wheel and whirl you around as He desires. Then as surely as God is God, and you are you, you will turn out as an exact likeness of the vision. But don't lose heart in the process.[22]

You see, I had my own goal. And when the fire ran out, I thought the time was up. I thought it was time to quit the process—to move on and try something else. But what kept me from running was knowing that God was the one who first spoke the vision into me. I remember that day. I will never not be able to trace the day and know, clearer than anything else, that God gave me an organization to steward, and now that I had to grow up and figure out how to steward it with these new feelings.

"You know you don't have to feel guilty," my psychiatrist told me when I took the feelings to her. "You don't have to feel guilty about not loving where you're at right now. There's no shame in that."

But wait . . . I am carrying all the shame. I am so ashamed.

To know my psychiatrist is to know that she speaks in a soft voice that makes you feel like everything is going to be okay. I will yap on nervously for ten minutes straight, and she will cock her head to the side like a beagle and say to me, "But what about Jesus?"

She is a voice of reason and of love, and she thinks the voices of condemnation that are firing in my brain need to shut up and stop being backseat drivers—and she tells me this with kind words.

"You don't have to carry those things," she tells me. "It's not the 'out of love' feeling that is running you into the ground—you know that, right? It's all the guilt you feel for feeling this way. Do you ever let God touch that?"

No. Of course not. Duh. Why would I ever let God touch the stuff that actually needs healing?

The answer is, I prefer to be buttoned up before God. I like to have it figured out and then get some confirmation or a little life lesson that I can treat like a souvenir. But no, I don't want to be messy before God.

The practical side of my brain does not know how to maneuver this suggestion. This suggestion of bringing things to God.

"How do I do that?" I ask her.

"You just sit with him. You ask the uncomfortable questions. And you wait. You test everything you hear. I recommend you keep a pen nearby because you're going to want to write some things down."

I leave her office and think about it all day. *How I'm going to get to the end of the day and I'll sit with Jesus. I am going to wait on him.*

I am not going to treat him like a vending machine. No, this will be a different feeling. Perhaps the feeling you get when you arrive at a friend's home and they ask you to help cook the meal. You chop veggies. You measure out the rosemary and the thyme. You're in the process of making something beautiful. You're not on the sidelines, waiting for the instant reward.

When the day winds down, I fix myself a cup of tea. I get comfortable in my favorite chair. I open my Bible and my journal. I write that first line, that first point of establishing communication. I take my psychiatrist's advice and just decide to be honest. To not hold back. To not speak pretty for a God who wants my ugly and unspeakable at any and all times.

I am resenting myself.

I am feeling shame.

I am feeling guilt.

I had no idea I had been carrying all these feelings for so long, letting them weigh me down day after day as I hid them from everyone.

And the most ridiculous thing happened. Peace. It flooded in. In a way I cannot fully explain, I experienced a crazy freedom by just admitting what was wrong. Things didn't magically shift.

I knew I'd have to keep coming back to the feelings. But I decided to do what my psychiatrist instructed me to do—to not shove down the feelings but to face them daily and say to them, "You are what you are. You don't define me though."

It became remarkably clear to me in the days ahead that God wasn't trying to take me backward; he was trying to propel me forward. But nothing could grow or change or develop until I stopped looking in the rearview mirror for the girl I used to be.

Love grows up. That's what happens in nearly every love story I've encountered. The fireworks infatuation doesn't go away so much as it becomes something different. It grows and develops. But if we don't steward the development, we might trick ourselves into thinking we've fallen out of love completely. What if the feelings are just trying to become more mature? What if the story isn't over—what if something newer, something deeper, is just beginning? I want to be open to that kind of growth. I want to continually step back into love when I feel off-kilter and step back into love when my feelings go awry. I want to say yes to a new level of love.

A new level of love takes time. It may mean going back to the basics for a while, going back to the daily tasks and disciplines that allow you to tend and care for that love. To water it daily. To give it new soil. To pay close attention to it. To say yes to the boring and mundane, just as much as you say yes to the crazy and the new.

A few years ago, Ann Voskamp wrote an article called "The Real Truth about 'Boring' Men—and the Women Who Live with Them."[23] In her ode to the boring men, she remarked about how her husband hadn't gotten down on one knee to propose to her. There was nothing extravagant, nothing choreographed, about the proposal or their marriage. She said she prayed that her boys would grow up to be men who didn't need the flashy because love is gritty, who realize it's not about getting down on one knee; it's about living your life on your knees.

I think this message extends beyond romantic love. For all the things we love—God, people, causes, missions, jobs we do, or hobbies we hone—there is the need to see that a commitment is pretty standard. It's black-and-white. It's not shiny; it won't always be impressive. It doesn't always have the jokes. But if we love these things enough, we'll keep showing up to prove they matter. We'll be able to ask ourselves, *What do I love enough that I am willing to keep stepping into that love when the feelings fade or morph into something I don't understand just yet?*

That's all I could do after God and I hashed things out. I knew, with clarity, that I wasn't done yet. That I needed to keep going and keep taking steps. That with each step, God was building something durable inside of me—something that would stretch out into all the other areas of my life. Now that I am partnered with myself instead of fighting against the guilt and shame of my feelings, I am open to that slow love changing me and making me stronger. I am saying yes to the sometimes boring love that makes me sturdy so I can be ready for more.

I cannot tell you it all feels magical. I cannot lie to you and tell you I always "feel it." I cannot say I never complain or that I don't quit six times in a day. All I can confirm is this: You learn so much about the long haul by just choosing to be in it on a daily basis. You learn how to uncover the everyday miracles in the midst of mundane tasks. You learn what your true yes is in a world that gives you endless options but doesn't teach you how to narrow those options down and say to one, "I'm sticking with you. You're it."

I am starting to see that I never fell out of love because I never fell in love to begin with. I stepped into love—it was a choice, and it still is—and I have been stepping into that love every day since.

That love is growing and changing all the time. And so are we.

Chapter 23

Fight for Rest

The lie you might believe for far too long is that rest is for the weak. Rest is for the lazy. Rest is for those who have time for it. But you? Well, you're out there making things happen so you cannot possibly take a break. Hustle harder. Move faster.

I spent almost all of my twenties never bothering to rest because of these lies above. I never took days off. I didn't know how to pump the brakes. I found so much of my identity in what I was doing that when I took time away, I felt like I wasn't myself or that I was missing out on precious hours where progress could be made. I thought if I stopped, everything would stop. I thought I was holding it all together. The truth was, I was just exhausted. I felt like everything relied on me. I was being a martyr for no apparent reason because I wasn't serving the world anything but a tired, worn-out version of myself. What I didn't see back then was that my choice to empty myself for the sake of "good work" wasn't heroic; it was a recipe for a deadly crash.

While I don't think the severe depression I experienced in 2014 was spurred on solely by failure to rest, I know that was part of it. It was an "all systems are down" sort of moment for my brain. The "do more, be more, work more, create more" mentality was broken at long last. When I found myself unable to use my brain, I could no longer hide behind my work. I could not continue to use it as an identity and I would have to make the long trip toward a new kind of normal, not knowing when the arrival at that new place would be.

At one point I visited a doctor who, if I am being honest, I didn't want to meet. I was at the point in the story where I was sick of doctors and sick of questions and I just wanted some answers. I just wanted someone to look at me from across their big desk, open up a drawer, and hand me back my old life. I was tired of being sick.

"So tell me about yourself," the doctor said to me.

I began to talk, wondering how I might be able to come off as normal as possible. But I remember only telling her the good parts, the successful parts. One after the other, I put accolades and accomplishments on the table as a way to say to her, *I'm okay. We don't have to do this weird doctor-patient thing. I'm doing just fine.*

And when I was finished, the woman just looked at me.

"Well, it all makes sense," she said to me, scribbling something in her notes. "I mean, you could have seen this train crash coming a mile away. At the rate you were going, there was no way you could not crash."

It was one of those statements that make you think—did other people see the train crash coming? Did I see the crash coming? How did I not see what this doctor sees and if I had seen it, couldn't I have prevented it?

These are questions I'll never have the answers to, but I do know just this: I was bound to crash at some point. If the standard of success and worth came from pleasing other people, I was bound to crash. If the only thing that could fill me was a checklist of things that made me look impressive, then, yes, there was bound to be a crash. And though I wish I could have seen the warning signs, the crash was necessary to wake me up.

When the crash came, I was forced to rest. To put it bluntly,

I was humbled into rest, since I could no longer be an independent go-getter. I had to look at myself and ask some tough questions. With the questions came some unavoidable realities to face.

I naively thought I was holding everything together. I thought if I took a break, things would crumble. Turns out, I am not holding the world together. That is not my job. It is not my job to control the people I love. It is not my job to always be successful. It is not my job to never fail or hit a wall or need to start again.

As long as I think I'm holding the universe together by working seven days a week and never taking breaks, I'm not trusting God. I am finding subtle ways to send out the message, "I cannot rest. I cannot take a break. I cannot stop because I'm afraid if I stop, everything will cease."

If that is the reality today, you need what I needed back then—a bigger God. A God who can handle my taking breaks. A God who gave me rest as a gift, not as a one-way ticket to the sidelines. I needed to re-meet the God of the Sabbath, and it was a painful but necessary road to travel to get there.

If I'm not careful, I know I could go right back to that place where I worship the hustle and the "do, do, do" more than my Creator. I know I still have it in me.

It doesn't help that it feels like two groups of people are at war these days when it comes to the topic of rest. One camp believes we don't need it at all—we can sleep when we're dead. The other camp thinks we need it too much—we can just freely devote our days to idleness.

I go back and forth, and I've decided I want to be in the middle camp, if such a middle camp exists. I don't want to be screaming or sleeping my life away. I want to be purposeful with my days, knowing it's not my job to make all the things happen before noon. I want to work hard and rest hard, knowing God is in both of those things.

My friend Jane always says that rest is the new hustle, and I agree with this. When we rest, we place our trust back in God by saying, "I know I don't control the universe. I am taking my hands off the steering wheel and trusting that you're enough to keep all things spinning."

One of the first things Jesus does for people is extend an invitation. He puts it very plainly to the people following him: "Are you tired? Are you burned-out? Are you absolutely done? Come to me, and I will give you rest. I can teach you how to live light and free."

He isn't mad over the exhaustion. He knows exactly where we are on the map and just how tired we feel. He sympathizes and invites us into something better. I can promise you it's something better than a to-do list that never ends and a story line that relies on our having to hold it all together.

It's a beautiful invitation, and a standing one, but it requires that we come forward. Rest isn't something we stumble on. It does not happen by accident. Rest is something we have to enter into and it's a pure gift. We cannot try to "perfect" it to please God. He is already pleased, and nothing we do or don't do can change that reality.

But regardless of the invitation, we have to pick the pause. We have to fight for rest. We have to be really intentional with when and where and how and how long. Otherwise we'll live in this cycle of:

Oh, things will slow down at the end of the year.

Things are about to get quiet.

Well, summer was busier than I expected, but I'm planning to take a break soon.

The excuses will keep coming forward if we allow their admission.

Anne Lamott says, "Almost everything will work again if you unplug it for a few minutes, including you."[24] The keyword is *unplug*. To make space. To say no to the excuses. To clear out the noise. To get into the silence, even if that only means we put our phones on airplane mode.

It wasn't until I'd lived in Atlanta for two full years that I took a real break. A mentor had suggested I go on a retreat nearly a year ago. He told me I would never be able to process all the shifts and changes happening in my life if I didn't slow down. You cannot hear God leading you if you always arrange for the noise to be louder than him.

I didn't listen to that mentor's suggestion. There was too much pressing all around me. I was convinced the world would fall apart if I stepped away for forty-eight hours.

But my roommate at the time bought me a plane ticket to Joshua Tree so we could camp out for a few days and I could experience camping in a national park, one of her favorite pastimes.

This time my autoresponder was up. I had no more excuses to dish out. Our campsite was miles and miles into the desert of California, no sign of a single bar of phone service even if I wanted there to be.

As we pulled up to the campsite—a small dirt space encased by jumbo rocks on three sides—the only thing there to greet us besides the cacti was the silence. It was a deafening kind of silence—the type that, at first, your brain doesn't know what to do with.

This kind of silence hadn't existed in my life up until this point.

I was forced to face myself, and the silence was shrill.

My mind raced for the first three hours and finally something broke open in me. I unraveled a little and told myself, *Relax. You have nothing to be afraid of.*

I used to be tempted to live a life covered by noise. Even as I prayed in the mornings, I found myself easily distracted by others. Tied to the stimulation was a bigger issue: I was finding validation—in the form of tweets and comments—more than I was finding it in God.

The praise never kept me satisfied. There was a fork in the road. I could either survive by the scraps of validation from fragile humans or feed at the table of God and stay full.

Silence brings to the surface what the noise manages to bury.

The question is this: Are you ever silent enough to face yourself? To face what you've needed to see for a really long time?

When we talk about rest, it's easy to get a picture in my brain of taking a catnap or finding time to do a cucumber melon face mask. Rest is often thought of as snuggling on the couch for a Netflix binge or going away on a vacation. But are we really recharging? Do we ever take a break from the noise that is at our fingertips and in our earbuds 24/7?

By the time night fell in that campground, I was hooked. I was absolutely enamored with the quiet, with the forgetting to check my phone, with the freedom to just be without any noise telling me who or how to be.

I was reading books by the fire. I was pouring words into my journal. I was laughing and crying and becoming inspired again. Peace met me there in the desert.

"I don't want to neglect seasons that grow me down into roots," I wrote. "I would like to always be building or always be laughing but Ecclesiastes 3 tells me there must also be the tearing down. There must also be weeping."

There is a time to speak, I read in that passage, and a time to be silent. As I traced those words, I stopped: *be silent.*

The Hebrew word for *silent* is *chashah.* It means "to be still."

Being still is the first step to planting roots deep down into God.

Solomon goes on to say in Ecclesiastes that we will never control the timing. The purpose of us being here—leading and loving and sharing—is not so we can become good at micromanaging people and dealing with noise. We could easily believe that lie and body-slam every hour into the calendar, but that is not the point. We are here to take on more of the person of Jesus, not more of the noise that sings to us about our fragile sense of self-worth.

As the bacon sizzled in the frying pan placed above a propane tank, I realized the world had not crumbled because I'd chosen to step away. The more glorious part? If the world did indeed crumble, then I would be none the wiser out here in the desert. You think you're going to miss out on everything when you turn off the phone, but you don't end up missing out at all—you gain more than you can imagine.

For the first time in such a long time, I could be engaged with my thoughts.

They weren't frantic. They weren't berating me to get back to work so I could prove my worth. I breathed in and knew, *I'm okay. God is here.*

And the most beautiful part? Entering into this peace came through just the simple decision to turn off my phone and get away for a few days. It wasn't extravagant. If it had been extravagant—a process that took a lot of time to get into—I would have surely made all the excuses to not rest. When Jesus talked about rest—setting aside a sacred day in the week for rest—he was very clear in telling people there was no need to get all legalistic about it. There is no right or wrong. That's not the point of taking a break.

Rest isn't a rule; it's a chance to reset. A chance to hear your thoughts again and know you're okay. A chance to come back to yourself and come back to your roots. It can be as simple as taking a few minutes out of your day to grab a latte or getting out in nature for a hike. Nature moves to a different rhythm and clock than we do—sometimes it's nice to tune in to nature's schedule. It could be reading a book instead of scrolling during the spare fifteen minutes you have. Rest can come from gathering ingredients and making a meal with your own two hands or picking one day a week to unplug from the rest of the world and return to yourself and the things you love—taking a nice nap, running a warm bath, having dinner with friends, enjoying a slow morning with nothing specific to do. Rest can be anything you do that omits the noise and steers you back to that still, small voice inside you.

If we can dull the roar around us, we can hear what a real voice sounds like. The voice that makes our fears cease. The voice that keeps us rooted and makes us braver than we can be on our own.

That voice will tell you who you are, and it will always sound like love. The noise of this world will never be able to do the same or show you the multitudes of purpose you possess within you. Twitter won't show you that. Instagram won't reveal it. Amazon won't deliver it. An empty inbox won't prove it.

When you take time to rest, you say yes to going back to basics—yes to who you were before the race to be "more" began.

Chapter 24

Build the Fire

Several years ago, my friend Nia and I decided to go camping.

Mind you, both of us had minimal camping experience when it came to the practical "camping" side of things, like lighting a fire or setting up a tent. I had always just relied on other people, I guess. From a Google search, Nia discovered you could use lint to build a fire, and she somehow obtained a tent that looked like it had barely survived World War II. We didn't realize we were choosing to camp on what would be the coldest weekend of the year in Georgia. Up until this point, I assumed Georgia didn't get cold, so I assured Nia, "We're going to be just fine."

I think we did everything wrong on the camping trip, apart from our food selection. We did a great job of selecting snacks, essentials to make s'mores, and other snacks, but we took too long to drive to our campsite. We stopped at tourist attractions. We grabbed dinner before heading into the woods. We went from a plan of getting to the campgrounds around 4:00 p.m., just in time to set up before nightfall, to not arriving until after dark. We had two headlamps, but we found out as we pulled up to the dark campground that only one worked.

We did a great job of picking a place that had little to no phone service—so if, God forbid, we needed help, we had no way of reaching anyone. We pulled up to a vacant site and began to make the trip back and forth to drop off our stuff. After one of the trips from the car, we came back to notice a Maglite flashlight in the middle of our campground that hadn't been there before. I've watched plenty of Lifetime movies, enough to know this is how most of them either start or end. It was official. This was the end of us.

As I plotted the end of our lives, a man emerged from the campsite beside us. He waved over at us and let us know he'd left the flashlight for us to use.

"I noticed you had only one headlamp, and it's pretty dark out here," he said. "I figured you could use some extra light!"

We thanked the good Samaritan for his kindness, and the flashlight was actually quite useful as we set up the World War II tent and prepared to build our fire. With a lack of service, we couldn't google "how to build a fire," and it turns out that neither of us really knew the "how" behind it.

Nia fiddled with matches and lint, but nothing caught fire. Like clockwork, the man at the campsite next to us walked over and asked if we needed some help. Within minutes, he created an expert fire for us, one that would last for a few hours. I wish I could remember the guy's name, but it escapes me. I swear to this day that he had two first names, so if you want to name him in your head for the sake of the story, let's just call him Timothy Anthony—the patron saint of fire building.

Timothy Anthony came back later in the evening and invited us to his fire, which was much nicer and bigger and more professional. We sat and chatted with him for a little while before we decided it was time to get some rest. In actuality, it was hardly late enough to go to sleep, but we were so cold that we decided the sooner we went to sleep, the sooner we'd forget about how we couldn't feel our bodies any longer.

In the morning, we awoke to Timothy Anthony building

our fire yet again. He'd also brewed coffee for us, so I figured at this point one of us would need to marry him. Everything was good and great with Timothy Anthony, and it only became weird when he went off on a rant about how California wasn't part of the United States. We politely agreed to disagree about US history, and then Nia and I bundled up to go on a hike.

We weren't expecting what happened next. Our patron saint of fire building had somehow managed to pack up his camper and vacate the premises during our hour-long hike. Almost like he was an angel sent to keep us alive in the woods, he disappeared as if he'd never been there all along.

A few hours later, though we'd paid for two nights of camping, Nia and I packed up the World War II tent, the little baggie of lint, and all our snacks and drove back to the city. Instead of the second night of camping, we ate biscuits at a brunch spot in town and then went to see a movie.

We could have stayed. We could have made something work. But we had a realization just an hour after our patron saint left us stranded at the campground: For as many times as he built our fire for us, he never taught us how to build the fire for ourselves—and we never thought to ask. We became content with this awesome fire when what we needed in order to be able to go off on our own, was the tools and the know-how to build our own fire.

I think this is the culture we live in today. With social media acting as lighter fluid, we become so enamored with the fires of other people that, if we aren't careful, we never learn how to build our fires. We never gather the tools. We never bundle up the sticks. We never struggle with the flint and the matches. We are simply complacent and content to watch everyone else build the biggest fires, and we feed off those fires as if they are enough for us.

The problem with this is that we never become independent. We live vicariously through the people who edit their lives to fit our screens. We miss out on the best part of the story when we focus on thinking other people's fires are enough to keep us going—the transformation that comes from doing rather than talking.

I want you to know about the fire you bring into this world and desperately want you to believe it matters, that this place wouldn't be the same without you. I want you to know that I cannot be you and she cannot be you and he cannot be you, and for that reason, you must play your part.

I don't want you to wake up and realize you've been a spectator all this time in the lives of others. I wish for you to be so deeply entrenched in this life that there is evidence of it beneath your fingernails and caught in your hair. I want you to love hard and fall down and create beautiful stuff and get goosebumps, but it requires you to live, to really live with all you have. It demands that you push back this fear that you bring nothing valuable to the table and that you silence the voices long enough to get your knees in the dirt and begin to work with the fire.

It's going to look quite different for me than it does for you. What you came here to do is different than your best friend, that girl on Twitter, or that person you envy. You've got your own gifts to give to a hurting and broken world, but you won't be able to put your everything into those gifts if you're always focused on the impact of other people.

One of my friends just moved to a new city, and I'm proud of her because she is listening to God. Really listening. I know this much is true because I asked her, "Why are you moving to Atlanta when you've only ever wanted to live in Nashville?"

"Well, God didn't tell me to move to Nashville. I heard it

really clearly that I was supposed to come to Atlanta, and so I'm here."

That takes some serious guts—to hear God and still choose to listen when you'd rather pick your own plan A. To hear God and think he might be handing you plan B because you cannot yet see that his plan A is better than yours.

So now she is here in Atlanta—across the country from everyone she knows, but finally, finally, God has her full attention. God has her right where he needs her, and he has been using this time to weed out the lies in her that she must be like _____ and must sing like _____. Where she used to doubt the things that set her apart, God is using this space in Atlanta to show her that those things are no accident— they're her edge.

If we don't take time to figure out what we bring to the table as individuals the world will miss out on what we could have done. It's no use to spend all our hours trying to clone the results of someone else when God wants to do something new with what's already inside us.

Are you open to God doing something new? This is what I have to ask myself when I'm scared or timid or think I could act like so and so and get more applause. *Am I open to God doing something new with me?*

It may not even be what you are expecting. I think we have this capacity to believe that if God is going to use us, it must be on some sort of stage or platform. At least that's how my brain used to think. As I've planted down roots and learned to love where I am in my story, I've found the most valuable things I do are for people in my closest circles—for the ones who will never tweet or share about it. These are the fires I'm addicted to building. When I make dinner for my family and it is healthy and filling and good for us, that's a fire set inside our bellies. When I clean my house, light some candles, and fill a wood platter with meat and cheese so that a group of mamas can have a night away from the chaos, that's a fire set in us to recharge and regroup together. When my friends show up at my door after a long day or send texts filled with prayers, that's a fire in me to keep going. I've stopped assuming the act of building a fire must be a public one where people clap and cheer. The best fires I've learned to build have been quiet and steady—they crackle and do their job of lighting the way for others, but they're not proud and they're not for everyone to stand by. Where I used to be fearful that these kinds of fires would never matter to me, now I set them daily and cannot get enough of the warmth they bring.

The anthem of the world is, "Be loud. Be bright. Be front and center." But God has a better anthem. I don't think God is interested in the level of applause we'll get or how the attention might fill our little egos. That's not his end goal. But I do think he placed unique things inside of all of us and is hoping we take the time to unlock them. Unlocking gifts that have lain dormant may take a while, but it's the sweetest thing. And I can only tell you from experience that I've never felt a closer communion with God than when I'm doing what I know he created me to do.

This may be a call to exploration. This may be a chance to try something new. It's perfectly okay to not be sure where the next path leads. This is the exciting part. Take your time figuring out what makes you feel most alive. Experiment for the sake of experimentation. Enjoy the process—God is in all of it. And when the voice bellows at you to step back instead of step in, turn down the volume. Turn down the volume, and lean all the way in.

And if I can add one more thing before you get out there with your sticks and flint (ditch the lint), know this: There will always be more fire to go around. There will always be more need for it. You don't have to live under a banner of scarcity; you don't have to think that if you share the tools you've gained, it means you'll be pushed to the sidelines so someone better can come along. Share your tools. Share your gifts. Share what you are learning, and don't hold back. Help people set little fires everywhere.

It only takes one glance at the nightly news to know that our world is in some mighty thick darkness now. People are scared and losing hope. People are searching for direction and purpose. Suicide rates are at an all-time high—so much of which is linked to the screens, the screens, the screens. But we can put down the phone at any time and step outside to live. We can find others who are struggling to see light or good in their own stories and coach them into building fires.

Here's what will happen if we get on the same page, if we decide to be people who listen to nudges and participate in the story rather than people who spectate, speculate, judge, or dismantle the stories of others through our words and actions: the world will have more light in it.

The only thing that has ever worked to combat such great darkness is light—and all this light starts with a little fire.

Chapter 25

Go Find Sarah

Years ago, I told my story at a youth conference, and it took everything inside me to not crawl out of my skin and go hide. I'm not my most comfortable with young people. I carry a real fear that I will be judged and mocked. I think it may be some unresolved angst from middle school that still haunts me. Whatever it is, I clam up around young people and find myself doubting my very existence.

The kids at the conference didn't smell good. They were at that age where someone had yet to hand them a stick of deodorant, but it desperately needed to happen. They were distant and halfway paying attention. I felt like the least interesting person in the world who'd somehow been given a microphone.

When I came off the stage, a few of the students came up to talk to me. When they cleared out, a girl was left standing there on her own. She had glasses and dark frizzy hair. She kept her head down as she approached me. She didn't put out her hand but told me her name was Sarah.

Before I could say anything, Sarah was rattling off a laundry list of things she felt ashamed of. I'm not good at this . . . and I hate myself for this . . . and one time I did this . . . and I self-harmed last week . . . and sometimes I don't even think I want to be here.

She fidgeted with her hands anxiously as she spilled out

word after word in what felt like a confession. I didn't know what to do. I didn't have Youth Conference 101 down to a science. I didn't know if I should get her to talk to someone or wave someone over. So I did the only thing I could think of at the time. I grabbed onto her shoulders and drew her in as close as I could. I got up to her ear, and in the loudest whisper I could use to get through to her, I spoke the two best words in the English language into her ear: *You're okay.*

These words have been in my family for years and years. They carry a strong meaning. We've discovered that these two words can dismantle hostility and bring someone to a place of calm. These two words—you're okay—are like a prayer, an anthem for the hurting and the broken. Something about these two words unleashes hope when they're said out loud and cracked open over someone. I speak the words *you're okay* to so many people in my life because I think there's magic to them. I think God lives in those two words.

"You're okay, Sarah," I repeated to her. "Stop looking for a reason to not be okay. You got up today. You made it here. You're okay."

And with that, Sarah broke. Suddenly I was standing there holding her in my arms as she sobbed loudly, not caring about any other students in the room. People watched, and I diverted my eyes from their eyes as I decided to rock this stranger in my arms until she was ready to let go.

I don't know how long we stood there. I don't know how many times I said "you're okay" over her. But I do know this: God was right there, and there was a feeling I couldn't shake, like, "We are going to make it. We are going to make it and be just fine."

I never saw Sarah again after that day, but I remember her

frequently, especially when I get caught up in wondering what the point of this whole life is. Yes, there are those days when everything seems too painful and so pointless. If I'm not careful, this feeling of meaninglessness can easily spread and give way to a fear that none of this matters, that maybe I'm an accident in a hopeless world.

If you've ever felt that fear on your skin or had it whispered into you in the middle of the night, I just want you to know you aren't alone. That fear isn't a crazy one—it's not one you have to be ashamed of. I think that fear rattles on the inside of many of us. I think so many of us are afraid that maybe we're the accident in the room.

But this is what I know about God, and it's a truth that has been crucial in fighting this fear every time it sprouts up: God is not a God of accidents. Nothing he does, nothing he created, nothing he allowed, is an accident. God is not a God who orchestrates accidents.

He isn't looking at our lives right now and thinking, *If you had just tried harder, I would have moved more. If you hadn't fallen for him or gone for her, I would have loved you more.* I think if there's one lie that Fear tries to wreck us with, it's the lie that God can't use us just as we are. The lie that we need to be more perfect to be used. The lie that we need to live a cooler life to be used. The lie that everyone else will be used and we'll be left on the sidelines.

For the longest time, I made the mistake of thinking that if a speaking engagement like the one at that youth conference was awkward, it meant it was an accident. That it would have been better to just stay home. If something was painful, it had to have been an accident. If something was messy, it was most definitely an accident and likely all my fault. But even through the mess of smelly teenagers, I met Sarah. I got to hold Sarah for a moment. And it meant something to me and I think it meant something to her, and so I can't say any longer that my presence was an accident.

Your questions—not an accident.

Your geography—not an accident.

Your darkness—not an accident.

Your pitfalls—not an accident.

Your relationship status—not an accident.

If you and I keep thinking that the occurrences and realities of our lives are accidental, we miss out on the very thing we want so badly—the chance to help others. We will miss that opportunity if we don't see that God wants to use us in the messiness. He wants to use us in the unfinished stories.

Where the world tells me to have my microphone on, fully cranked and ready for any documentable moment, the voice of God is soft and sure as it reminds me when I start to panic about how I will prove myself, "You don't have to hustle or push. You can be patient. Grow humbler. Find your place on the back burner, and put others first. There you will discover a life that is rich and full. Drop the mic; this isn't all about you."

But here's the thing—Fear always has a chance to come back with a vengeance if I'm not paying attention to that soft, sure voice. If I scroll too much, if I talk instead of pray, if I observe the lives of others and wonder why mine doesn't look like theirs, the old tune comes back into my brain, and suddenly I'm stuck thinking once again that I am missing pieces.

So I go back to the drawing board. I approach Fear again. I rinse and then repeat this truth:

I am not accidental.

I am not disqualified, too young, or too old.

I am not in some story that demands perfection before I can start my race.

I have everything I need to get out there and shine.

My God supplies my every need. I don't need to acquire new supplies or worry about how loud the audience claps. I just need to keep my eyes on him. I have what it takes. I trust the God who is in me.

And as I rinse and repeat and rinse and repeat these words, I find out that I am not missing pieces. I am not a five-hundred-piece puzzle gone awry. In actuality, I am missing people. When I get too focused on the fear of missing pieces, I am missing the chance to be a light to a hurting world.

What if you aren't missing pieces but you're simply missing people?

What if you're missing Sarah? If Sarah showed up today, would you see her? Would you draw her in and whisper the words we all need to hear sometimes?

There are Sarahs out there who need you to see them. I am sure of it. They don't need you to have all the right answers or to always get it right yourself. Some people just need to know they're not alone. Some people need that gift you have to offer—the one you keep buried out of fear that you're not good enough. Some people need those words of encouragement you have brewing in your soul—those words could spread like wildfire and be a healing balm to hurting people if you would just let them out. And some people need something so simple but so hard to give at times—your presence. They need you to sit alongside them and listen to their story. They need you to not flinch or run the other way. They need you to nod your head and say, "Me too," or they need you to repeat until they start to believe it, "You're okay.

You're okay.

You're okay.

You're okay.

None of this is an accident. You're needed here. Drop the microphone, and go find Sarah.

Chapter 26

Finish Well

Several years ago, I attended a gathering my friends and I liked to call "Girls Night." The funny thing about these nights is that they were started by two guys who were complaining about how girls always got together and talked about deep stuff, but the same standard wasn't held for guys. They wanted more deep conversations. So they started having nights when a question would be asked at the very beginning—a deep question about something like singleness or religion or kindness—and then the conversations would take on a life of their own for the next few hours as we encouraged one another, debated, and talked the issue out. We'd be sitting there until one in the morning, doing life together.

On one of those nights, we talked about our friend who wanted to date but felt like he couldn't find a girl to connect with. With the help of Twitter and a vetting process, we found a girl on Twitter who was willing to go on a blind date with him. This all happened in the span of an hour.

You know how they say "it takes a village"? Well, a village prepared that man for his first date with this girl from Twitter. We helped him say the right things. We helped him plan the date. We gave him the thumbs-up to bring her flowers. We made him call instead of text. We pep-talked and prepped him because we wanted him to believe in himself, and the whole thing ended up being an experiment in dating in the twenty-first century. Our hypothesis became, *What might happen if he took all the right steps to be a gentleman and dated this girl the way you dated someone back in the 1950s?*

The first few weeks went great. I was starting to think something would come out of it. He liked her; she liked him. He planned fun dates. He kept things interesting. He even had this one date where they went to a coffee shop and got hot chocolate and then went to a bookstore where they walked around and read favorite lines and stories to one another. Everything was going well, and he was ending every date by asking, "Can I see you again soon?"

He was blunt. He was honest. There was no ghosting or breadcrumbing or orbiting—or any of the phrases we use to describe dating in today's society.

But then DJ hit a low. He'd been so diligent to make his dates with this girl intentional, but she started making excuses for why she couldn't hang out. Suddenly she had other plans or was out of town or was starting to get sick. He felt defeated because it didn't take a rocket scientist to figure out that maybe she didn't want to date him anymore. He wanted to give up and just stop texting altogether.

I was fine if he wanted to end things, but what I didn't want him to do was duck out on the story early. Even though he was indeed being ghosted, I didn't want him to step away and script his own ending. When we leave a story too soon, we sometimes end up scripting an ending that isn't true—and it isn't usually a favorable one. More often than not, it's one about how we weren't enough for that person in the end. It's a false ending that wants to hold us back rather than propel us forward. If we don't watch the stories we tell ourselves, they can end up becoming beliefs about ourselves that are hard to shake free of, narratives about how we are unwanted or unseen.

"You are not giving up until you properly end it," I told him. "You are not going to punk out at mile 3 and write yourself an ending to this story that isn't true. You're going to finish."

Here's what I know about mile 3: At 11:59 at the end of the old year in Times Square, a nearly twelve-thousand-pound sphere of crystal begins to drop 141 feet in 60 seconds as a million people cheer and kiss, while millions more watch from their living rooms. But less than a mile away, at the same stroke of midnight, several thousand people dressed in tutus and crowns take off running on a four-mile race around Central Park. For many years, I've been a part of that crowd. At midnight, my friends and I would start running with the five thousand other people. I'd plug in my best playlist and spend those miles reflecting on the last year and running into the next year.

Right around the three-mile mark is when someone like me, who is not a runner, starts to get tired. My legs start to get sore, and a few cramps start to form. This would be the moment when it would be easier to quit or to simply walk the rest of the way. Walking that last mile would still be a victory, but I am surrounded by people who are running, and I want to keep going too.

However, the planners of this race must know that the three-mile mark is where people like me start to lose a little stamina and need a pick-me-up. A reason to keep going.

Seemingly out of nowhere, white tables lining the roadway emerge, and dozens of individuals in New Year's crowns are waiting to pass out little Dixie cups filled with sparkling apple cider. They're cheering you on. They're letting you know you've got one mile left. It's the perfect moment to stop, cheer on your friends, and continue toward the finish line. You say Happy New Year to the people passing out the Dixie cups, and you keep going because you know the real truth. You are going to make it. You are going to finish. You've got this.

"You don't punk out at mile 3," I said again to DJ. "That's the best part. That's where the cheerleaders show up with the little Dixie cups of sparkling apple cider! It's not time to give up. You have to keep going."

In the end, DJ decided to finish how he started. He sent a text to the girl he'd been dating and asked for an honest answer. Was she feeling it or not? The girl did eventually text him back and give him the answer he deserved: she felt they weren't compatible and that they should go their separate ways but that she was so thankful about how intentional he'd been the whole way through.

DJ wasn't crushed or even discouraged when he read the text. He experienced something we all deserve when we like someone else—closure. When there's closure, it's easier to take your eyes off that door and look forward to a new one opening.

That night, after DJ's closure text arrived, I showed up at church to meet him with a $3.99 bottle of sparkling apple cider I got at the grocery store, along with a stack of cups because the store was out of little Dixie cups.

Together in the parking lot, we rejoiced and clinked the sparkling apple cider over stories with true endings, modern-day romances, choosing not to give up at mile 3, and the chance to finish in the same way we started: Strong. Strong. Stronger.

I don't know about you, but I want to finish well. I want to be known for how I finish gracefully and completely rather than becoming the person who always starts a new venture but never stays long enough to see the fruit of finishing.

I don't think the issue is necessarily starting things. I see people start things every day. New programs. New wellness journeys. New classes. New one-hundred-day challenges. When you get past the initial fear of putting yourself out there to potentially fail, you can start almost anything.

One of my favorite authors, Jon Acuff, wrote a whole book called *Finish* as a sequel to another book he wrote called *Start* because he realized he got the wrong message. People didn't need help starting something. Starting is the easy part once you get going. It's the finishing—when the momentum is in the rearview mirror and only you can see the finish line (and even that view is pretty foggy)—that is hard. To finish when the world doesn't see the daily progress. To finish when there's no one chanting your name.

This all seems so clear to me, and yet I still expect God to give me more when I have yet to finish things I know need to be finished well. It's easy to look at everyone else and think, *Well, I want to be doing that too.* It's easy to run five races at once, but it doesn't guarantee that any one of them will be finished well or in time. If we aren't careful, we start well and finish poorly. We tire out and limp across the finish line, licking our wounds and ordering streamers off Amazon for our pity party. But it doesn't have to be that way. We can finish in a different manner: Strong. Empowered. Grateful for the experience. Ready for what comes next.

People will remember how you finish, how you steward the things on your plate, and how you close a door on one thing to walk into the next. I can promise you that. People will remember if you dropped off the face of the planet before the project was over or if you left the church you were attending regularly and never told anyone you were leaving. People won't always remember how you started, but they keep track of finish lines. I don't bring this up to imply that it's your job to finish well to prove other people right or wrong, but people do watch. They watch to find examples. They watch to see who they would like to become. They watch to see if you'll allow Fear to script the ending or if you'll step into a bigger glory.

There are very few things in this world we will ever be able to control. We don't get to pick when seasons end or when people leave us. We don't get much say over whether a television show is canceled or a report comes back as "cancer-free." We don't get to dictate the weather or force people to do things they don't want to do. We get very little control, but I am adamant in believing there are two things we do get to control: how we show up and how we finish.

It may be a hard conversation you've been putting off because you know it will change the relationship. It may be a doctor's appointment you need to make but you're too scared to move forward. It may be something you're training for and every part of you wants to quit right now. If you quit now, you will miss out on the sense of completion that comes from going out on a limb to invest in yourself and then seeing the investment pay off in real, tangible results.

What if you shifted the focus toward the finish line and went after it with everything you had? What would change? What kind of victory would you possess? How much more would God do with you, knowing you're the type of person who always finishes what you start?

The finish line is up ahead. Are you ready? Are you set? Go on then; run on through to the other side.

Chapter 27

Operate from the Overflow

If you ever want to take an honest look at yourself with no filters or ways to mask what's really there, date someone and go on to marry them.

I'm convinced marriage gives us the most real mirror into ourselves. Marriage will drag up from the murky waters all your worst qualities and put them on display so you can be properly horrified by the things you think, say, and feel daily.

I can attest to this because I am married to the literal kindest man in the world. He doesn't have a mean bone in his body. He never says an unkind word about anyone. He's constantly working to improve himself, and he serves without asking for anything in return. Since day one of our relationship I've been facing myself and the jacked-up beliefs about love I bring to the table—and let's just say the process has been eye-opening.

The first thing I noticed was our approach to food. As Lane and I began dating, we visited different restaurants. When the meal came out, he always wanted me to try the food. He prepared generous bites for me, and if I liked something, he didn't mind sharing nearly half with me. I, on the other hand, showed how stingy I truly am. I gave him small bites. I coveted the dish in front of me. I made comments like, "Don't eat it all—that's mine," when it came to tacos and burgers and basically everything.

After several conversations, we realized we grew up in different kinds of households. Both of those households held love in them, but while he grew up sharing everything with his siblings and believing there would always be enough, I grew up having to fight for what was "mine" in the refrigerator and pantry. I remember big fights over who ate whose what. There was always tension about what belonged to whom.

It's funny how these small beliefs can grow up to be something much bigger when you reach adulthood. Lane clearly looked at life from a lens of abundance, and I was always fearful of scarcity, of running out, of not having enough. Those lenses extended themselves into our views about God.

Lane has a healthy view of God. He believes God is good and kind and is on his side at all times. He believes, because the Bible says so, that God doesn't change. Who God was yesterday is who God will be tomorrow. As for me, up until the last few years, I carried around a fear-driven mentality about God. I was constantly afraid I would be forgotten. That somehow I'll mess up the plan of humanity, and God will say, "Sorry, girl, I had such big plans for you, but I had to hand them off to someone else who was more put together than you." Whereas Lane sees a God of abundance, I've had to wrestle with why I'm so quick to think that God is a God of table scraps and limited resources.

I once had a friend who told me that when you love them, you must take them at 100 percent. You cannot love them properly if you love them at 80 percent with the hope that 20 percent might change. You're either at 100 percent or you aren't.

I think the same is true for my beliefs about God. I either take him at 100 percent and believe in a God who is merciful and kind and gives more grace. Or I take God at 10 percent and think he is stingy and small and more like a Polly Pocket than my Guide or my Savior.

But scarcity is a liar.

So here's the prayer I learned to pray: "God, be bigger than my fear." If my fear is too big, so toxic that it takes over the entire story line, then my God is too small, and I need to rehearse what I know about him until abundance wins the story line back again.

When I think about true abundance, I think about my neighbor Ms. Pat. This woman has what appears to be all the makings of a secret garden right in her front yard. I know most people put a garden in their backyard for privacy, but not Ms. Pat. She stands outside every single day and proudly waters her whole front yard.

A few months ago, I was sitting on my front porch reading when Ms. Pat came walking down the street toward me. It was eight in the morning, so I wasn't expecting any interaction at that hour, but Ms. Pat walked up and asked me if I wanted any flowers.

I figured it wasn't polite to say no to flowers, no matter the hour of the day. I thought a big vase of flowers on our dining room table would be nice.

"Sure!" I told her.

She motioned for me to follow her and started walking back down the street toward her house. As we entered her front yard, Ms. Pat pulled a big shovel off the ground and began to dig up plants all over the yard. She dug down to the root and pulled up the plants, handing them to me one at a time.

"I thought," I said. "I mean . . ." I had heard her wrong. I anticipated she was giving me freshly picked flowers. I didn't think she was handing me plants yet to bloom that would require me to replant them and tend to them.

"Now," she said to me, "when you plant these in the ground, they are going to come back year after year."

"I don't want you to dig up your garden for me though," I told her. "That's not what I wanted you to do."

She looked at me, cocked her head to the side like she was mildly confused, and then said matter-of-factly, "I have overflow though. When you have overflow, you can't not share it."

My mind sort of exploded at those words. How firmly she spoke them. How much she lived by this belief: *Yes, I have been given much, and so I'm not going to fear running out. I'm going to give out of the overflow I've experienced.*

It's a fight to reorient your brain, especially if you've looked at life through a lens of scarcity for a really long time. It's a fight to quiet the fear that wants to say "mine," to overcome the tendency to keep squirreling away all you've been given for a future apocalypse.

But there's no time like the present to start living out of the overflow, even when you can't see it at first. I can't say I'm an expert at abundance yet (or that I'll ever be), but I can tell you the one thing I started to do to fight for that abundance over the lies of scarcity in my life: I started thinking of others more and myself less.

Not in an exhausting or unhealthy way. Not in a "stretching myself too thin" way. I just started being more open with my calendar, more open with my resources, more open with what I've been given. Little by little, God is opening up my tightly clenched hands and teaching me that this is how I stay in the fight for an abundant life.

The more I give myself away, the more I'm figuring out there is no lack. On the days when I just "can't," someone else can. On the days when I can give, there are plenty of people with needs. Overflow doesn't mean only I have enough; it means I shift my eyes to see that together, with all of us in the story, there is enough, but it requires that we share.

You and I have a chance to operate out of the overflow. My favorite story in the Bible illustrates a life like that. At the beginning of Jesus' ministry, he walks into Peter's house and performs a miracle by healing his mother-in-law of a high fever. The Bible says that Jesus touched her hand, and the fever broke. But the next line is the one that gets me: "she got up and began to wait on him."[25]

She didn't wait. She didn't hesitate. She didn't sit it out in fear that the fever would come back. She didn't question the miracle. She simply got up, right where she was, and began to serve in all directions, out of gratitude and out of the overflow.

I've read this story about Peter's mother-in-law more than a hundred times, but what I love about God is that you can read one of his stories a hundred times and still find something different, something you never saw before, on the hundred-and-first time through.

It's in Mark's version of the story, right after Jesus heals Peter's mother-in-law. That same evening, when the sun went down, people started showing up from everywhere to receive healing and hope. The text reads, "The whole town gathered at the door."[26]

The result of the miracle that began with Peter's mother-in-law was the catalyst for the entire city to huddle up, link arms, and stand at the door together—hoping for a better story.

Just like this woman who rose up and got to work, we can adopt her attitude at any point in the story. The posture of overflow. The posture of "more than enough." The posture where we open up our hands and start serving out of the abundance.

I believe there is a hurting and tired city at the door right now that needs hope and light, love and service. It starts with our being willing to get up at once and begin to serve. It starts with our retiring the anthems that we are "benched" or "on the side-lines" and putting our skin in the game as we enter a bigger story. This bigger story requires a different anthem, a better fight song.

I cannot imagine a more beautiful picture than this, but I know it's the kind of story I want to live day by day.

One where we trust the gifts God has given us.

One where we hone the gifts in darkrooms and through practice.

One where we cheer people forward with our road signs and with our presence.

One where we don't focus on finishing for the sake of our own finish lines, but one where we link arms and help one another cross over into what's coming next.

Fight Forward:
A Final Song for You

Over the last few years, as I've lived the material in this book, I've learned this isn't the type of story you can wrap up tidily with a bow and put on the shelf. I don't think I've "arrived" at a finish line so much as I've gathered the tools to fight forward and better every time Fear shows up with yet another heartless anthem customized for me. I hope that this book will be one you can come back to as you grow and change and show up to this lifetime.

I've wrestled with how to send you off with one last fight song for the road ahead. No doubt, you will move into some bright and beautiful things in the years to come. There will be golden opportunities and once-in-a-lifetime happenings that I hope you'll savor and take pride in. There will also be the temptation to listen to Fear in the background, crackling like a vinyl. But the truth is, you already know the better anthem. You already have the fight song deep inside you. It is embedded there. Now your mission is simple: Learn the words of this better anthem by heart. Tattoo them on your life. Speak them into other people. Live the words out through action, and people will naturally come to see there's something different about you.

Years ago, after emerging out of the depression, I remember talking with a friend about how God had woven miracles into the messiness when he stopped and stared at me with this weird gaze. He paused a moment longer before saying, "I see it in your eyes. I see that you fought to the other side, and you're a different person now. It's in your eyes."

This was sweet confirmation for me, and I want to declare the same thing over your life: you can fight to the other side and become a different person.

You are never too far gone. You are never beyond repair. God can always take the ruins and rebuild on top of them. You are worthy of new things that have yet to be accomplished, and I believe you will see those things with your own two eyes.

There may be times when you fall off the path, stumble over the lyrics, or lose your way, but you are the child of a God who sings the words back into you on the days when you don't remember them. You are not defined by the bumps in the road or the detours. You are made stronger because of these things. You can dismantle the lies. You can speak to Fear and make it back down because God has put that power inside you.

You can be that cheerleader on the side of the road for someone who is afraid no one will show up. You can wave your sign and pump your fist and call out the greatness as you see it in others. You can run a ridiculously impactful race, and you can lean on God as your power source for all the miles. You have all of it inside you, waiting to be tapped.

As for me? I'll be right over here with my glittery handmade sign that reads in obnoxiously big letters, "YOU'VE GOT THIS." I'll be standing right there, cheering for you until my lungs give out. I can't wait to see the finish lines you cross and the fires you start all over this world.

So head on out of here.

Get moving.

Above all else, keep fighting forward.

Acknowledgments

Before I ever wrote a word of this book and the concept was just a "one day" thought in my mind, I knew there would be a section carved out for the cheerleaders. I know the power that comes from being supported and becoming a support to others. I am who I am because of the cheerleaders in my own life. The ones who stood by me through the good and the ugly. The ones who made the metaphorical glittery signs (and sometimes the literal ones) and lined the roadside, holding them up, pumping their fists in the air, and cheering me on through every milestone of my writing career. It is my prayer that you will find people as good as the people I am about to thank and that they'll surround you at every new bend in the road.

As always, my first bit of gratitude belongs to God. I am so thankful that he continually fills me with stories to write down. If you find more of God's goodness in the world after reading this book, then my work is done, and done well.

To Laney—your constant support and belief in me are what drive me to show up to this work every single day. Thank you for never allowing me to shrink from my calling. Thank you for filling me with fight songs on a daily basis through your acts of service and love. Also, thanks for the endless quesadillas and nightly ritual of preparing the coffee for me. I, Tuesday, and Novalee are the luckiest in the world to have you.

Acknowledgments

To Mom and Dad—so many of the words in this book ring true because of how you raised me and taught me to be unapologetic for what I bring to the table. Because of you and the way you made sure I never lacked anything, I know how to share my gifts and always make room at the table for more people to join.

To Baccu—can you believe it? Another book to add to your collection. I wish you could be here to hold them in real life, but I know the celebration will be that much sweeter when I see you again. This book, as well as every other book I write, is for you.

To my family—thank you for covering me in prayer and being the biggest cheerleaders in the stands. I am forever grateful for your unending support.

To Dawn, Hayley, Linda, Hoke, Taylor, and Brian—thank you for prepping me for every writing session and celebrating me every time that last sentence hit the page. You are my best friends, and I've loved walking through new seasons with you by my side. Taylor, the next book is definitely about conspiracy theories.

To my Monday Night girls—thank you for the roses, for the laughs after a long writing day, for the Lucky Charms mixed with popcorn, and for teaching me many of the lessons packed into this book. I'm thankful for each of you in my life.

To Christina—your wisdom was everything to me during one of the toughest seasons of my life. Thank you for telling me to take up more space.

To Felicia—thank you for always inviting me on walks. I can always trust that life will make more sense and God will be more real to me when we finish each three-mile loop.

To Melissa—I don't think I would have survived this writing season (or 2020) without your voice memos. I am so, so thankful we get to cheer one another on every day.

To Shelley, Louie, and my PCC family—thank you for giving me a home to worship in since the first day I moved to Atlanta. I am who I am because of the way the church has backed and supported me. You go the extra mile, and that shows me how to do the same for others.

To Mackenzie—thank you for the constant advice, support, and friendship. Above all, thank you for believing in the ideas I come up with and helping me make those ideas a reality. You are an answer to prayer.

To Stephanie—I'm grateful to God that my job in this lifetime is to write books with you as my editor. It's the biggest privilege and honor for me. Thank you for making me a better writer and for being the fiercest cheerleader backing my words.

To the team at Zondervan—I cannot thank you enough for putting your energy and belief behind my books. I am consistently amazed by the ways you show up and make me feel seen and known throughout every step of the process. I'll keep making you proud.

To the MLL team—thank you for joining me every single day in this good fight to change the world and make it a bit brighter with the work you do. I am so lucky to be running alongside each of you.

There are simply too many people to thank—in Atlanta, Connecticut, and beyond—who sent me coffee, uttered prayers, delivered meals, and dished out fresh pep talks to keep me going. You know who you are, and I'm infinitely grateful for your selfless acts of love in my life.

And to my readers—I cannot adequately express how grateful I am to know you're in my corner. Each of you is a force to be reckoned with. I wrote every one of these fight songs with you at the forefront of my mind. Nothing would make me prouder than to see you get out there and run your best race with fervor and gratitude. I will never stop cheering you on. Put down this book—it's time to make waves with this life you've been given.

Notes

1. See James Clear, *Atomic Habits: An Easy & Proven Way to Build Good Habits & Break Bad Ones* (New York: Penguin, 2018), 164–65.
2. J. K. Rowling, "The Fringe Benefits of Failure, and the Importance of Imagination," Harvard Commencement Speech, June 2008, https://news.harvard.edu/gazette/story/2008/06/text -of-j-k-rowling-speech.
3. Psalm 23:5.
4. Anne Lamott, *Operating Instructions: A Journal of My Son's First Year* (New York: Anchor, 1993), 135.
5. D. Martyn Lloyd-Jones, *Spiritual Depression: Its Causes and Its Cure* (Grand Rapids: Eerdmans, 1965), 20–21.
6. Quoted in Sonia Thompson, "Why Tons of Failure Is the Key to Success, According to Seth Godin," Inc., December 7, 2016, www.inc.com/sonia-thompson/why-tons-of-failure-is-the-key-to -success-according-to-seth-godin.html.
7. Song of Songs 2:15.
8. Oswald Chambers, *So Send I You / Workmen of God: Recognizing and Answering God's Call to Service* (Grand Rapids: Discovery House, 2015), 21.
9. See Saint Augustine, *The City of God*, trans. Marcus Dods (1871; repr., Peabody, MA: Hendrickson, 2009), 460–61.
10. Johann Hari, "Everything You Think You Know about Addiction Is Wrong," TEDGlobalLondon (June 2015), www .ted.com/talks/johann_hari_everything_you_think_you_know _about_addiction_is_wrong.

Notes

11. "What Is Discouragement?" Institute in Basic Life Principles, https://iblp.org/questions/what-discouragement.

12. Isaiah 45:19 NLT.

13. Oswald Chambers, *My Utmost for His Highest: An Updated Edition in Today's Language* (1935; repr., Grand Rapids: Discovery House, 1995), September 30.

14. Paul David Tripp, *Suffering: Gospel Hope When Life Doesn't Make Sense* (Wheaton, IL: Crossway, 2018), 21.

15. See 1 Kings 17:2–6.

16. Elizabeth Gilbert, *Eat, Pray, Love: One Woman's Search for Everything Across Italy, India, and Indonesia* (London: Bloomsbury, 2006), 158.

17. Galatians 5:7.

18. Judith Orloff, *Emotional Freedom: Liberate Yourself from Negative Emotions and Transform Your Life* (New York: Harmony, 2010), 306.

19. Galatians 5:13.

20. Exodus 14:14.

21. Psalm 42:6 MSG.

22. Oswald Chambers, *My Utmost for His Highest: An Updated Edition in Today's Language* (1935; repr., Grand Rapids: Discovery House, 1995), July 6.

23. Ann Voskamp, "The Real Truth about 'Boring' Men—and the Women Who Live with Them," HuffPost, November 11, 2013, www.huffpost.com/entry/the-real-truth-about-bori_b_4296073.

24. Anne Lamott, "12 Truths I Learned from Life and Writing," TED2017 (April 2017), www.ted.com/talks/anne_lamott_12 _truths_i_learned_from_life_and_writing/transcript.

25. Matthew 8:15.

26. Mark 1:33.

Come Matter Here

Your Invitation to Be Here in a Getting There World

Hannah Brencher

From viral TED Talk speaker and founder of The World Needs More Love Letters, Hannah Brencher's *Come Matter Here* is the book you need to start living like you mean it here and now.

Life is scary. Adulting is hard. When faced with the challenges of building a life of your own, it's all too easy to stake your hope and happiness in "someday." But what if the dotted lines on the map at your feet today mattered just as much as the destination you dream of?

Hannah thought Atlanta was her destination. Yet even after she arrived, she found herself in the same old chase for the next best thing . . . somewhere else. And it left her in a state of anxiety and deep depression.

Our hyperconnected era has led us to believe that life should be a highlight reel—where what matters most is perfect beauty, instant success, and ready applause. Yet as Hannah learned, nothing about faith, relationships, or character is instant. So she took up a new mantra: Be where your feet are. Give yourself a permission slip to stop chasing the next big thing, and come matter here. Engage the process as much as you trust the God who lovingly leads you.

If you're tired of running away from your life or of running ragged toward the next thing you think will make you feel complete, *Come Matter Here* will help you do whatever it takes to show up for the life God has for you. Whether you need to make a brave U-turn, take a bold step forward, or finish the next lap with fresh courage, you will find fuel and inspiration for the journey right here.

Available in stores and online!

ZONDERVAN®
.com